CRITICAL-CREATIVE
WRITING

CRITICAL-CREATIVE WRITING

TWO SIDES OF THE SAME COIN

A FOUNDATION READER

Edited and introduced by

Michelene Wandor

Matador
9 Priory Business Park,
Wistow Road, Kibworth Beauchamp,
Leicestershire. LE8 0RX
Tel: 0116 279 2299
Email: books@troubador.co.uk
Web: www.troubador.co.uk/matador
Twitter: @matadorbooks

ISBN 978 1 8004 6505 3

British Library Cataloguing in Publication Data.
A catalogue record for this book is available from the British Library.

Typeset in 11pt Minion Pro by Troubador Publishing Ltd, Leicester, UK

Matador is an imprint of Troubador Publishing Ltd

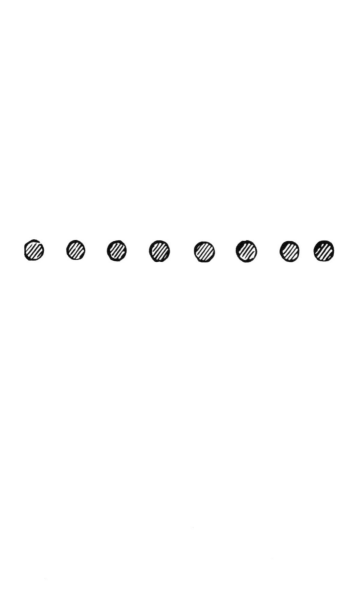

CONTENTS

It is only when the intellect is consciously directed to an examination of what the human mind produces, that we have criticism. There is a general impression that the same mind cannot do both the producing and the examining – that a mind is either creative or critical; or, in other words (to give scientific colour to the theory), it is either synthetic or analytic. The fundamental fallacy in the theory is that analysis is opposed to synthesis, the idea being crystallised by the employment of metaphors borrowed from the physical world – one is a tearing down, the other is a building up.

The fact is, however, that in mental operations analysis and synthesis presuppose each other; analysis, indeed, presupposing synthesis to a much greater extent than is the case in the reverse relation. Mere tearing apart is not analysis, for analysis implies a point of view; and the point of view is the synthesizing element. There is, therefore, absolutely no psychological basis for the absolute opposition between the creative and the critical mind.

David Klein, *Literary Criticism from 'The Elizabethan Dramatists: Repertory and Synthesis* (Sturgis & Walton, 1910, pp. xi-xii)).

INTRODUCTION

In the past few years, British universities, polytechnics, schools and even kindergartens have seen a massive growth occur in a subject that not too long ago was regarded as a suspect American import, like the hamburger – a vulgar hybrid which, as everyone once knew, no sensible person would ever eat. It is called Creative Writing, and along with other latter day or postmodern activities like Media Studies and Women's Studies, has turned into one of the subjects of the season. Besides achieving academic recognition, it has spread freely through the broader hinterland. Farmhouse seminars, weekend courses, evening writing workshops, postal courses and handy mercantile handbooks encourage all of us to develop the obscure quality known as creativity or stimulate the belief that we can all soon be running off with the Booker prize...

(Malcolm Bradbury, *The Times Literary Supplement.* January 17, 1992.)

In 2000, the British Council listed 40 postgraduate Creative Writing (CW) degrees in the UK. In 2003, a report produced by the English Subject Centre pointed to CW as a 'rapidly expanding province of activity'.[1] In 2004 there were about 85 undergraduate English degree courses, where CW was a component.[2] At the time of writing this Introduction (2021), according to UCAS, the university clearing house for student admissions, there were 187 CW postgraduate and 562 undergraduate courses available. There are a few full CW undergraduate degrees, but more commonly, CW is combined with English. It has also become an option within a range of other subjects, from history to medicine.

It is clear from this expansion that CW is a success story in the academy. It has generated its own literature and pedagogic practices. It has a symbiotic, if sometimes vexed, relationship, with English Literature studies. The relationship between the reading and writing of imaginative literature is now pretty well accepted as axiomatic. However, the separate and interwoven histories of English and CW have meant that the latter developed at different times, and in different ways.

English Literature and the academy[3]

In the US and the UK, arguments for studying literature in the vernacular (ie, English) language, were part of a move to challenge the dominance of the study of the 'classical' literatures of Greece and Rome. 'London was the first University to introduce English and English literature into its examination system. University College was founded in 1826, Kings in

---

1   *Creative Writing: Good Practice Guide* by Siobhan Holland. Report Series No 6, February, 2003.

2   'Forget the muse, it's hard graft you need.' Michelene Wandor, *Times Higher Education Supplement,* August 6, 2004, p.22.

3   For a fuller account, see Wandor, Michelene, *The Author is not Dead, Merely Somewhere Else; Creative Writing Reconceived* (Palgrave Macmillan, 2008).

1829…In 1859…for the first time, English literature appeared in a BA course.'[4]

The validation of English as a subject of university study in the UK was supported by the University Extension movement. From the 1860s, Oxford, Cambridge and London University teachers organised extra-mural classes to provide further education for working people, those who may have had very little schooling. As the 19th century wore on, the UE movement argued '…with greater and greater indignation, that Oxford was gradually becoming the only institution in which English Literature played no part. The subject of English came into the Civil Service exams, it was among the papers set for the Oxford and Cambridge Local examinations…Above all, in the new Extension Lectures, so warmly approved of by the public, English literature was more widely followed than Science or History.'[5]

In the US, as D. G. Myers has pointed out, the arrival of English Literature in universities involved a combination of reading and critical study of literature, and courses in teaching academic writing – these were called Composition and Rhetoric, and are still taught today:

> *The story of creative writing began with the opposition to philology and resumes with the effort in the 1880s and 1890s to restore literary and educational value to the teaching of rhetoric…English composition was the first widely successful attempt to offer instruction in writing in English…it was formulated at Harvard in the last quarter of the century out of a constructivist belief that the ideal*

4   Stephen Potter, *The Muse in Chains* (Jonathan Cape, 1937), pp.141–142.

5   Ibid, p. 185. See also Anthony Kearney, *The Louse on the Locks of Literature* (Scottish Academic press, 1986), pp.36–37.

end of the study of literature is the making of literature...
English composition established the autonomy of college
writing and created a demand for courses in writing from
a literary and constructivist point of view. And these were
necessary preconditions of creative writing's acceptance as
a subject of serious study...Until about the 1920s, though,
there was small need for creative writing per se because
English composition and creative writing were one and the
same thing.[6]

Teaching more directly vocational writing in the US came
with the first journalism course in 1908. Teaching imaginative
writing – CW proper – developed rapidly; the influential Iowa
Writers' Workshop was established in 1922–3. Its system of
workshop-based teaching has influenced CW pedagogy all
over the world.

In the UK the trajectory and time scale of CW were rather
different. The University Extension movement's classes focussed
on literary 'appreciation', rather than writing. In the universities,
appreciation developed into literary criticism, but, unlike in
the US, without any teaching directed at writing practice. This
difference between the US and the UK goes some way towards
explaining why CW took longer to be established in the UK.

Creative Writing in the UK

During the 1950s and 1960s, novelist Malcolm Bradbury
visited and taught in American universities, where he was aware
of the existence of CW courses. In 1965 he took up a post at
the University of East Anglia (UEA) in Norwich, one of the

---

6   D. G. Myers, *The Elephants Teach* (Prentice-Hall, 1996).

new universities built in the 1960s. UEA helped to pioneer interdisciplinary and comparative literature degrees, with their School of English and American Studies, in 1968. Bradbury became Professor of American Literature in 1970. In the same year, he and fellow novelist, Angus Wilson, set up the first MA in Creative Writing in the UK.

Their MA had two agendas: first, it combined the reading and study of literature, with the writing of literature. Secondly, it was intended as a cultural intervention in what Bradbury and Wilson perceived as a crisis in the high-art British novel, as compared with its livelier American counterpart. In other words, their desire was to encourage new, younger writers to produce vigorous, new writing. The radical departure in academic terms was that, following the example of the Iowa Writers' Workshop, students were able to submit a 'creative dissertation' for their final MA degree.

The establishment of UEA's MA signalled the arrival of CW in the academy, and its structure showed an understanding that reading and writing are (or should be, or must be) two sides of the same coin. This meant that 'traditional' Eng Lit academics began to explore the teaching of imaginative writing, alongside bringing in professional (and would-be professional) writers to teach their art/craft.

Undergraduate CW followed. In 1984, dissatisfied with traditional English teaching, Susanna Gladwyn began incorporating imaginative writing into her classes, with immediate success. Gladwyn was in touch with the Verbal Arts Association, chaired by poet and teacher, Anne Cluysenaar, and formed after a 1982 seminar on 'The Arts and Higher Education', funded by the Calouste Gulbenkian Foundation. A group of professional writers and radical academics (including

Raymond Williams and Richard Hoggart) called for 'Urgent reforms... in the teaching of English if the practice of verbal arts is not to remain for most people a missing subject'. The VAA's patrons included writers William Golding, Doris Lessing, Ted Hughes and Iris Murdoch. Susanna Gladwyn ran the first full CW undergraduate degree, called 'Writing and Publishing', at Middlesex University in 1991–2.

Creative Writing Pedagogy

Creative Writing has generated its own, now extensive, literature and pedagogical practices. The literature consists of a combination of how-to handbooks, and collections of essays by writers explaining how they approach their writing. The practical teaching methodology is largely built round the 'workshop', where students read their and each others' creative work, which is then subject to peer and tutor criticism – 'feedback'. There can be ancillary links to more 'academic' elements in other subjects – on research, publishing or aspects of literary and cultural study.

Students write 'commentaries' to accompany their creative work. These are called various names: self-reflective commentary, supplementary discourse, critical commentary, exegesis. They might include personal, individuated documentation: diaries, journals, work diaries/logbooks, along with discussions of writerly issues, their own practice, their literary context, and relevant 'theories' or theorisations, concerned with imaginative writing. For undergraduates, the final commentary might be 200–500 words, for MA up to 5,000 words, for PhD from 10,000 words, to half the final word length. Assessment weighting could vary from 10% of the final mark, up to 50%

at PhD level. Students were/are rarely required to pass both 'creative' and 'critical' elements, showing that the 'creative' is valued more highly than the 'critical'.

In 2003, the English Study Centre surveyed 'Supplementary Discourses in Creative Writing Teaching' (Project Supervisor Dr Robert Sheppard). The survey concluded that there was 'little uniformity over the value, principles, aims, techniques, level descriptors, or assessment patterns and weighting, or even amount, of this writing'. There was little shared understanding across the academy of the conceptual and cultural foundations necessary to inform students' accounts of their own writing processes, as well as the more scholarly, research-based literary critical elements.

However, in 2008, the National Association of Writers in Education (NAWE) produced the first specific Benchmark Statement for Creative Writing teaching and research in higher education. In 2016, NAWE, together with the Quality Assurance Agency for Higher Education (QAA), produced an official Benchmark Statement, and this was updated in 2021. These are guidelines, and individual universities and tutors compose their courses in a variety of ways.

Undergraduates taking creative writing modules as part of their English degrees, are more likely to be au fait with the conventions of textual criticism/close reading and developments in critical thought, than many (if not most) postgraduate students, with writing ability and potential, but no grounding in literary education. It is common for students to be accepted onto postgraduate CW courses on the basis of their imaginative writing, not their educational history or qualifications. In terms of access to such art/craft study, this latter may be laudable, but it creates its own pedagogic problems.

In the case of both critical commentary and workshop practice, there is one abiding question: from where do students gain their knowledge of critical terminology, and/or a genuine understanding of the literary conventions within which they are working, let alone literary criticism and theory? For those with no prior experience of critical reading or literary analysis, it's a matter of what they pick up in the workshop, or from aleatoric aspects of tutor supervision, or simply by dint of engaging with writing and response during their course. However, whatever this yields, it is likely to be piecemeal, rarely intellectually challenging, or considered that responses to imaginative writing are merely 'subjective'. Critical thinking, an understanding of the history and practice of literary criticisms of different kinds are not available to them. Ways of thinking about writing, attempts to develop 'theories' of writing (conventions, 'rules', even) are rarely or automatically joined up.

This Reader

This Reader brings together many of the key elements in the symbiotic relationship between the reading and writing of imaginative literature in the academy. They are two sides of the same coin, although it took until well into the 20th century for them to be united. The anthology is also the final part of a trilogy of my critical/creative writing. *The Author is Not Dead, Merely Somewhere Else; Creative Writing Reconceived* (Palgrave Macmillan, 2008) charted the histories of English and CW in the academy, with a thoroughgoing analyses of its principles and aims, and a critique of workshop practice. *The Art of Writing Drama* (Methuen, 2008) analysed the characteristics of drama as a written form, and challenged some of the predominant practices of teaching a performance-based genre.

My own imaginative (I avoid using the term 'creative' – since writing non-fiction is also, in a very real sense, 'creative') writing has always ranged over poetry, prose fiction and drama. I've written the latter for theatre and radio, with the occasional foray into television. I've also reviewed the arts, in print and on radio, written books and articles on music, gender and writing and women and drama. I am one of a large number of writers whose experience and income has been boosted by the arrival of CW in the academy. My CW teaching has ranged from playwriting in an adult education class, to drama students, and in a number of universities in all three imaginative genres. Like many professional writers, I had no previous experience of teaching, and to some extent, had to make it up as I went along, developing a pedagogic approach which turned out to be rather different from the dominant workshop method. Hence the above two books, and this Reader.

This Reader is not Theory (with a capital 'T') for Creative Writing. It is distinctive (if not unique) in that it bridges the gap between the practical handbooks for CW, and the many anthologies of literary and cultural Theory, which have developed from a combination of philosophy, sociology, politics and linguistics. While these latter anthologies can have relevance to the techniques and tropes of imaginative writing, they very rarely form part of CW courses. Mediating between these two extremes, this Reader presents carefully selected historical extracts, from the Old Testament to the borders of Theory.

It charts the ways writers and thinkers have considered imaginative writing through the centuries. Their aims and purposes have been varied; from a desire to understand how imaginative literature travels from the mind to the page, to trying to define 'rules' and conventions, and much more. For example, the Readings travel from Aristotle and the three unities, to the beginnings of the concept of 'genre'; through the Renaissance, with its appeal back to classical rubrics and rhetoric, into the 18th century, with 'genre' as we now know it; then, via the belle-lettrism of the 19th century, the development of literary criticism, notions of 'style', value judgement, and finally, to Theory.

The Reader can be used in whatever way the autocritical, autodidacticism of lecturers and students decide, in their different CW contexts. It will provide historical and linguistic depth to many of the familiar mantras (cliches, even?) of CW. For example, one of CW's most repeated rubrics, 'write what you know' might be explored through the conceptual line from the graven images of the Old Testament, via Aristotelian mimesis, to Romantic notions of individual emotional expression, and to categories of realism and naturalism. As something of a non-exclusive, non-exhaustive guide, each extract is followed by a cluster of 'keywords'. Readers may – and should – perceive and list others for themselves. The aim of the anthology is to enhance thinking about writing, and thinking about thinking about writing, and, of course, to encourage further reading.

Conclusion

In 2004, I interviewed Anne Cluysenaar, pioneer of undergraduate CW at Lancaster and Sheffield Hallam universities. She set up a three-part degree course of linguistics, stylistics and creative writing.[7] Further back in history, across the Atlantic, as part of the Iowa Writers' Workshop, Norman Foerster, critic and historian, was '…hired in 1930 to assume control of the newly established School of Letters at the University of Iowa…creative writing at Iowa was never intended to become a free-standing apparatus of courses, an autonomously constituted "workshop", leading to a separate degree. It was to be only one branch of study in the literary tradition designated for all types of students – teachers, critics, scholars and writers…The school's curriculum was to be a sequence of courses in noncontemporary texts and authors, criticism, literary history, and even the history and structure of the English language. Creative writers would do scholarship; scholars would creatively write.'[8]

These ideals have not yet permeated the bedrock of CW pedagogy. I hope this Reader will help enable that to happen.

Michelene Wandor

---

7   Personal interview with author, 2004.

8   Myers, pp. 124, 133.

PART ONE

Hebrew, Greek and Roman

THE OLD TESTAMENT

GENESIS: *Chapter 1*

1. In the beginning God created the heaven and the earth.
2. And the earth was without form, and void; and darkness was upon the face of the deep. And the Spirit of God moved upon the face of the waters.
3. And God said, Let there be light; and there was light.
4. And God saw the light, that it was good: and God divided the light from the darkness.
5. And God called the light Day, and the darkness he called Night. And the evening and the morning were the first day...

26. And God said, Let us make man in our image, after our likeness: and let them have dominion over the fish of the sea, and over the fowl of the air, and over the cattle, and over all the earth, and over every creeping thing that creepeth upon the earth.
27. So God created man in his own image, in the image of God created he him; male and female created he them.

creation; author; gender; mimesis; creativity

EXODUS: *Chapter 20*

4. Thou shalt not make unto thee any graven image, or any likeness of any thing that is in heaven above, or that is in the earth beneath, or that is in the water under the earth...

abstract art; anti-mimesis; creativity; art

PLATO (c. 428–427 BC)

_____

ION *(translation by Benjamin Jowett)*

SOCRATES: I often envy the profession of a rhapsode, Ion; for you have always to wear fine clothes, and to look as beautiful as you can is a part of your art. Then again, you are obliged to be continually in the company of good poets…And no man can be a rhapsode who does not understand the meaning of the poet. For the rhapsode ought to interpret the mind of the poet to his hearers, but how can he interpret him well unless he knows what he means?…

ION: Very true, Socrates; interpretation has certainly been the most laborious part of my art…

SOCRATES: …all good poets, epic as well as lyric, compose their beautiful poems not by art, but because they are inspired and possessed. And as the Corybantian revellers when they dance are not in their right mind, so the lyric poets are not in their right mind when they are composing their beautiful strains: but when falling under the power of music and metre they are inspired and possessed; like Bacchic maidens who draw milk and honey from the rivers when they are under the influence of Dionysus but not when they are in their right mind. And the soul of the lyric poet does the same, as they themselves say; for they tell us that they bring songs from honeyed fountains, culling them out of the gardens and dells of the Muses; they, like the bees, winging their way from flower to flower. And this is true. For the poet is a light and winged and holy thing, and there is no invention in him until he has been inspired and is out of his senses, and the mind is no longer in him: when he has not attained to this state, he is powerless and is unable to utter his oracles. Many are the noble words in which poets speak concerning the actions of men; but like yourself when speaking about Homer, they do not speak of them by any rules of art; they are simply inspired to utter that to which the Muse impels them, and that only... and he who is good at one is not good at any other kind of verse: for not by art does the poet sing, but by power divine. Had he learned by the rules of art, he would have known how to speak not of one theme only, but of all; and therefore God takes away the minds of poets, and uses them as his ministers, as he also uses diviners and holy prophets, in order that we who hear them may know them to be speaking not of themselves who utter these priceless words in a state of unconsciousness, but that God himself is the speaker, and that through them he is conversing with us...For in this way the God would seem to indicate to us and not allow us to doubt that these beautiful poems are not human, or the work of man, but divine and the work of God; and that the poets are only the interpreters of the Gods by whom they are severally possessed...

SOCRATES: ...When you produce the greatest effect upon the audience in the recitation of some striking passage, such as the apparition of Odysseus leaping forth on the floor, recognised by the suitors and casting his arrows at his feet, or the description of Achilles rushing at Hector...are you in your right mind? Are you not carried out of yourself, and does not your soul in an ecstasy seem to be among the persons or places of which you are speaking, whether you are in Ithaca or in Troy or whatever may be the scene of the poem?

ION: That proof strikes home to me, Socrates. For I must frankly confess that at the tale of pity my eyes are filled with tears, and when I speak of horrors, my hair stands on end and my heart throbs...

SOCRATES: And are you aware that you produce similar effects on most of the spectators?

ION: Only too well; for I look down upon them from the stage, and behold the various emotions of pity, wonder, sternness, stamped upon their countenances when I am speaking...

performance; interpretation; intention; inspiration; memory; possession; audience; madness; the unconscious; empathy; identification; spectator/reader; criticism; judgement; the Muse; prophets; divinity; soul; pity; wonder

THE REPUBLIC *(translation by Benjamin Jowett)*

Book Three

…You are aware, I suppose, that all mythology and poetry is a narration of events, either past, present or to come?

…And narration may be either simple narration, or imitation, or a union of the two?…You know the first lines of the Iliad…the poet is speaking in his own person; he never leads us to suppose that he is any one else. But in what follows he takes the person of Chryses, and then he does all that he can to make us believe that the speaker is not Homer, but the aged priest himself. And in this double form he has cast the entire narrative of the events…when the poet speaks in the person of another, may we not say that he assimilates his style to that of the person who, as he informs you, is going to speak?

…And this assimilation of himself to another, either by the use of voice or gesture, is the imitation of the person whose character he assumes?

…Then in this case the narrative of the poet may be said to proceed by way of imitation?

…If Homer…instead of speaking in the person of Chryses, he had continued in his own person, the words would have been, not imitation, but simple narrative…Or you may suppose the opposite case – that the intermediate passages are omitted, and the dialogue only left.

…In saying this, I intended to imply that we must come to an understanding about the mimetic art – whether the poets, in narrating their stories, are to be allowed by us to imitate, and if so, whether in whole or in part, and if the latter, in what parts; or should all imitation be prohibited?

narration; description; dialogue; prose fiction; drama; first-third person; mimesis; point of view; drama

Book Five

We acknowledged – did we not? That different natures ought to have different pursuits, and that men's and women's natures are different...

I said: Suppose that by way of illustration we were to ask the question whether there is not an opposition in nature between bald men and hairy men; and if this is admitted by us, then, if bald men are cobblers, we should forbid the hairy men to be cobblers, and conversely?...

And if, I said, the male and female sex appear to differ in their fitness for any art or pursuit, we should say that such pursuit or art ought to be assigned to one or the other of them; but if the difference consist only in women bearing and men begetting children, this does not amount to a proof that a woman differs from a man in respect of the sort of education she should receive, and we shall therefore continue to maintain that our guardians and their wives ought to have the same pursuits.

gender; inequality; equality; division of labour

Book Ten

Of the many excellences which I perceive in the order of our State, there is none which upon reflection pleases me better than the rule about poetry.

...To the rejection of imitative poetry, which certainly ought not to be received...I do not mind saying to you, that all poetical imitations are ruinous to the understanding of the hearers, and that the knowledge of their true nature is the only antidote to them.

...Let us take any common instance; there are beds and tables in the world – plenty of them, are there not?

....But there are only two ideas or forms of them – one the idea of a bed, the other of a table.

...And the maker of either of them makes a bed or he makes a table for our use...but no artificer makes the ideas themselves...There is another artist...he who is able to make not only vessels of every kind, but plants and animals, himself and all other things – the earth and heaven, and the things which are in heaven or under the earth; he makes the gods themselves...And yet there is a sense in which the painter also creates a bed?

...Well then, here are three beds: one existing in nature, which is made by God...another which is the work of the carpenter...And the work of the painter is a third...Beds, then, are of three kinds, and there are three artists who superintend them: God, the maker of the bed and the painter...Would you call the painter a creator and a maker?

...And the tragic poet is an imitator, and therefore, like all other imitators, he is thrice removed from the king and from the truth?

…And what about the painter? I would like to know whether he may be thought to imitate that which originally exists in nature, or only the creation of artists?

…Which is the art of painting designed to be – an imitation of things as they are, or as they appear – of appearance or of reality?

…Then the imitator… is a long way off the truth, and can do all things because he lightly touches on a small part of them, and that part an image. For example: A painter will paint a cobbler, carpenter or any other artist, though he knows nothing of their arts; and if he is a good artist, he may deceive children or simple persons, when he shows them his picture of a carpenter from a distance, and they will fancy that they are looking at a real carpenter.

…The poet is like a painter who, as we have already observed, will make a likeness of a cobbler though he understands nothing of cobbling; and his picture is good enough for those who know no more than he does, and judge only by colours and figures.

…And now tell me, I conjure you, has not imitation been shown by us to be concerned with that which is thrice removed from the truth?

…And the same objects appear straight when looked at out of the water, and crooked when in the water; and the concave becomes convex, owing to the illusion about colours to which the sight is liable. Thus every sort of confusion is revealed within us; and this is that weakness of the human mind on which the art of conjuring and of deceiving by light and shadow and other ingenious devices imposes, having an effect upon us like magic.

…And the arts of measuring and numbering and weighing come to the rescue of the human understanding – there is the beauty of them – and the apparent greater or less, or more or heavier, no longer have the mastery over us, but give way before calculation and measure and weight?

…And this, surely must be the work of the calculating and rational principle in the soul?

…Imitation imitates the actions of men, whether voluntary or involuntary, on which, as they imagine, a good or bad result has ensued, and they rejoice or sorrow accordingly…the higher principle is ready to follow the suggestion of reason?

…And the other principle, which inclines us to recollection of our troubles and to lamentation…we may call irrational, useless and cowardly?

…And does not the latter – I mean the rebellious principle – furnish a great variety of materials for imitation? Whereas the wise and calm temperament, being always nearly equable, is not easy to imitate or to appreciate when imitated, especially at a public festival when a promiscuous crowd is assembled in a theatre…

…Then the imitative poet who aims at being popular is not by nature made, nor is his art intended, to please or to affect the rational principle in the soul; but he will prefer the passionate and fitful temper, which is easily imitated?

…we must remain firm in our conviction that hymns to the gods and praises of famous men are the only poetry which ought to be admitted into our State. For if we go beyond this and allow the honeyed muse to enter, either in epic or lyric verse, not law and the reason of mankind, which by common consent have ever been deemed best, but pleasure and pain will be the rulers in our State.

imitation; mimesis; knowledge; truth; representation; intertextuality; soul; imagery; material reality; the function of

art/literature; beauty; research; value judgement; science versus art; illusion; danger of art; passion versus reason; gender: male/ rational, female/irrational; empathy/identification/sympathy; popularity; reality; science

ARISTOTLE (384-322 BC)

POETICS *(c.330 BC) (translated by S. H. Butcher (1850-1910)*

1.

I propose to treat of Poetry in itself and of its various kinds, noting the essential quality of each; inquire into the structure of the plot as requisite to a good poem: into the number and nature of the parts of which a poem is composed...

Epic poetry and Tragedy, Comedy also and Dithyrambic poetry, and the music of the flute and of the lyre in most of their forms, are all in their general conception modes of imitation. They differ, however, from one another in three respects – the medium, the objects, the manner or mode of imitation, being in each case distinct...

There is another art which imitates by means of language alone, and that either in prose or verse – which verse, again, may either combine different metres or consist of but one kind – but this has hitherto been without a name...People do, indeed, add the word 'maker' or 'poet' to the name of the metre, and speak of elegiac poets, or epic (that is, hexameter) poets, as if it were not the imitation that makes the poet, but the verse that entitles them all indiscriminately to the name. Even when a treatise on medicine or natural science is brought out in verse, the name of the poet is by custom given to the author; and yet Homer and Empedocles have nothing in common but the metre, so that it would be right to call the one poet, the other physicist rather than poet...

poetry; genre; analysis; structure; imitation/mimesis; rhythm; harmony; form; author; prose; epic; tragedy; comedy

2.

Since the objects of imitation are men in action, and these men must be either of a higher or a lower type (for moral character mainly answers to these divisions, goodness and badness being the distinguishing marks of moral differences), it follows that we must represent men either as better than in real life, or as worse, or as they are. It is the same in painting...The same distinction marks off Tragedy from Comedy; for comedy aims at representing men as worse, Tragedy as better than in actual life.

imitation; action; morality; tragedy; comedy

3.

There is still a third difference – the manner in which each of these objects may be imitated. For the medium being the same, and the objects the same, the poet may imitate by narration – in which case he can either take another personality as Homer does, or speak in his own person, unchanged – or he may present all his characters as living and moving before us.

These, then, as we said at the beginning, are the three differences which distinguish artistic imitation – the medium, the objects, and the manner. Sophocles is an imitator of the same kind as Homer – for both imitate higher types of character; from another point of view, of the same kind as Aristophanes – for both imitate persons acting and doing. Hence, some say, the name of 'drama' is given to such poems, as representing action...

imitation; medium; narration; first/third person; drama; subject matter; style; form; heroes (sic); action; evocation; character; point of view; poetry

4.

Poetry in general seems to have sprung from two causes, each of them lying deep in our nature. First, the instinct of imitation is implanted in man from childhood, one difference between him and other animals being that he is the most imitative of living creatures, and through imitation learns his earliest lessons; and no less universal is the pleasure felt in things imitated. We have evidence of this in the facts of experience. Objects which in themselves we view with pain, we delight to contemplate when reproduced with minute fidelity: such as the forms of the most ignoble animals and of dead bodies. The cause of this again is, that to learn gives the liveliest pleasure, not only to philosophers but to men in general; whose capacity, however, of learning is more limited. Thus the reason why men enjoy seeing a likeness is, that in contemplating it they find themselves learning or inferring, and saying perhaps, 'Ah, that is he'. For if you happen not to have seen the original, the pleasure will be due not to the imitation as such, but to the execution, the colouring or some such other cause.

Imitation, then, is one instinct of our nature. Next, there is the instinct for 'harmony' and rhythm, metres being manifestly sections of rhythm. Persons, therefore, starting with this natural gift developed by degrees their special aptitudes, till their rude improvisations gave birth to Poetry.

Poetry now diverged in two directions, according to the individual character of the writers. The graver spirits imitated noble actions, and the actions of good men. The more trivial sort imitated the actions of meaner persons, at first composing satires, as the former did hymns to the gods, and the praises of famous men…

Whether Tragedy has as yet perfected its proper types or not; and whether it is to be judged in itself, or in relation also to the audience – this raises another question. Be that as it may, Tragedy – as also Comedy – was at first mere improvisation.

Aeschylus first introduced a second actor; he diminished the importance of the Chorus, and assigned the leading part to the dialogue. Sophocles raised the number of actors to three, and added scene-painting. Moreover, it was not till late that the short plot was discarded for one of greater compass, and the grotesque diction of the earlier satiric form for the stately manner of Tragedy. The iambic measure then replaced the trochaic tetrameter, which was originally employed when the poetry was of the satiric order, and had greater affinities with dancing. Once dialogue had come in, Nature herself discovered the appropriate measure. For the iambic is, of all measures, the most colloquial; we see it in the fact that conversational speech runs into lines more frequently than into any other kind of verse; rarely into hexameters, and only when we drop the colloquial intonation…

origins of poetry; imitation; instinct; gender; learning; pleasure; rhythm; iambic; tragedy; comedy; drama; dialogue; morality; harmony; experience; pain/pleasure; metre; high and low art; imagination; recognition; audience response

6.

…Tragedy, then, is an imitation of an action that is serious, complete, and of a certain magnitude; in language embellished with each kind of artistic ornament, the several kinds being found in separate parts of the play; in the form of action, not of narrative; through pity and fear affecting the proper purgation of these emotions.

Again, Tragedy is the imitation of an action; and an action implies personal agents, who necessarily possess certain distinctive qualities both of character and thought; for it is by these that we qualify actions themselves, and these – thought and character – are the two natural causes from which actions spring, and on actions again all success or failure depends. Hence the Plot is the imitation of the action: – for by plot I here mean the arrangement of the incidents. By Character I mean that in virtue of which we ascribe certain qualities to the agents. Thought is required wherever a statement is proved, or, it may be, a general truth is enunciated. Every Tragedy, therefore, must have six parts, which parts determine its quality – namely, Plot, Character, Diction, Thought, Spectacle, Song.

But most important of all is the structure of the incidents. For Tragedy is an imitation, not of men, but of action and of life, and life consists in action, and its end is a mode of action, not a quality. Now character determines men's qualities, but it is by their action that they are happy or the reverse. Dramatic action, therefore, is not with a view to the representation of character: character comes in as subsidiary to the actions. Hence the incidents and the plot are the end of a tragedy; and the end is the chief thing of all. Again, without action there cannot be a tragedy; there may be without character. The tragedies of most of our modern poets fail in the rendering of character; and of poets in general this is often true...Again, if you string together a set of speeches expressive of character, and well finished in point of diction and thought, you will not produce the essential tragic effect nearly so well as with a play which, however deficient in these respects, yet has a plot and artistically constructed incidents. Besides which, the most powerful elements of emotional interest in Tragedy – Peripeteia or Reversal of the Situation, and Recognition scenes – are part of the plot. A further proof is, that novices in the art attain to finish of diction and precision of portraiture before they can construct the plot. It is the same with almost all the early poets.

The Plot, then, is the first principle, and, as it were, the soul of a tragedy. Character holds the second place. A similar fact is seen in painting. The most beautiful colours, laid on confusedly, will not give as much pleasure as the chalk outline of a portrait. Thus Tragedy is the imitation of an action, and of the agents mainly with a view to the action.

Third in order is Thought – that is, the faculty of saying what is possible and pertinent in given circumstances. In the case of oratory, this is the function of the political art and of the art of rhetoric...Character is that which reveals moral purpose, showing what kind of things a man chooses or avoids. Speeches, therefore, which do not make this manifest, or in which the speaker does not choose or avoid anything whatever, are not expressive of character. Thought, on the other hand, is found where something is proved to be or not to be. Or a general maxim is enunciated.

Fourth among the elements enumerated comes Diction; by which I mean, as has already been said, the expression of the meaning in words; and its essence is the same both in verse and prose.

Of the remaining elements Song holds the chief place among the embellishments.

The Spectacle has, indeed, an emotional attraction of its own, but, of all the parts, it is the least artistic, and connected least with the art of poetry. For the power of Tragedy, we may be sure, is felt even apart from representation and actors. Besides, the production of spectacular effects depends more on the art of the stage machinist than on that of the poet.

imitation; action; narrative; catharsis; structure; dialogue; character; agent; thought; order; situation; moral purpose; tragedy; diction; life; pity; fear; reversal; recognition; emotion; motivation; plot

7.

These principles being established, let us now discuss the proper structure of the Plot, since this is the first and most important thing in our Tragedy.

Now, according to our definition, Tragedy is an imitation of an action that is complete, and whole, and of a certain magnitude; for there may be a whole that is wanting in magnitude. A whole is that which has a beginning, middle, and an end. A beginning is that which does not itself follow anything by causal necessity, but after which something naturally is or comes to be. An end, on the contrary, is that which itself naturally follows some other thing, either by necessity, or as a rule, but has nothing following it. A middle is that which follows something as some other thing follows it. A well constructed plot, therefore, must neither begin nor end at haphazard, but conform to these principles.

plot; structure; beauty; tragedy; action; order

8.

Unity of plot does not, as some persons think, consist in the unity of the hero. For infinitely various are the incidents in one man's life which cannot be reduced to unity; and so, too, there are many actions of one man out of which we cannot make one action…As therefore in the other imitative arts, the imitation is one when the object imitated is one, so the plot, being an imitation of an action, must imitate one action and that a whole, the structural union of the parts being such that, if any one of them is displaced or removed, the whole will be disjointed or disturbed. For a thing whose presence or absence makes no visible difference, is not an organic part of the whole.

unity; structure; plot; hero; action; imitation; subtlety of character

9.

It is, moreover, evident from what has been said, that it is not the function of the poet to relate what has happened, but what may happen – what is possible according to the law of probability or necessity. The poet and the historian differ not by writing in verse or prose...The true difference is that one relates what has happened, the other what may happen. Poetry, therefore, is a more philosophical and a higher thing than history: for poetry tends to express he universal, history the particular. By the universal I mean how a person of a certain type will on occasion speak or act, according to the law of probability or necessity; and it is this universality at which poetry aims in the names she attaches to the personages... In Comedy this is already apparent: for here the poet first constructs the plot on the lines of probability, and then inserts characteristic names – unlike the lampooners who write about particular individuals. But tragedians still keep to real names, the reason being that what is possible is credible: what has not happened we do not at once feel sure to be possible: but what has happened is manifestly possible: otherwise it would not have happened.

...Of all plots and actions the epeisodic are the worst. I call a plot 'epeisodic' in which the episodes or acts succeed one another without probable or necessary sequence...

But again, Tragedy is an imitation not only of a complete action, but of events inspiring fear or pity. Such an effect is best produced when the events come on us by surprise; and the effect is heightened when, at the same time, they follow as cause and effect. The tragic wonder will then be greater than if they happened of themselves or by accident; for even coincidences are most striking when they have an air of design.

documentary; imaginative; probability; universal; the particular; plot; episodic; credibility; cause and effect; superiority of poetry; history; possibility; necessity; comedy; tragedy; fact and fiction

10.

Plots are either Simple or Complex, for the actions in real life, of which plots are an imitation, obviously show a similar distinction. An action which is one and continuous in the sense above defined, I call Simple, when the change of fortune takes place without Reversal of the Situation and without Recognition.

A Complex action is one in which the change is accompanied by such Reversal, or by Recognition, or by both. These last should arise from the internal structure of the plot, so that what follows should be the necessary or probable result of the preceding action. It makes all the difference whether any given event is a case of *propter hoc* or *post hoc*.

simple/complex plot; recognition; reversal; action; imitation

11.

Reversal of the Situation is a change by which the action veers round to its opposite, subject always to our rule of probability or necessity...

Recognition, as the name indicates, is a change from ignorance to knowledge, producing love or hate between the persons destined by the poet for good or bad fortune. The best form of recognition is coincident with a Reversal of the Situation...Even inanimate things of the most trivial kind may in a sense be objects of recognition. Again, we may recognise or discover whether a person has done a thing or not. But the recognition which is most intimately connected with the plot and action is, as we have said, the recognition of persons. This recognition, combined with Reversal, will produce either pity or fear; and actions producing these effects are those which, by our definition, Tragedy represents. Moreover, it is upon such situations that the issues of good or bad fortune will depend. Recognition, then, being between persons, it may happen that one person only is recognised by the other – when the latter is already known – or it may be necessary that the recognition should be on both sides...

Two parts, then, of the Plot – Reversal of the Situation and Recognition – turn upon surprises. A third part is the Scene of Suffering. The Scene of Suffering is a destructive or painful action, such as death on the stage, bodily agony, wounds and the like.

recognition; reversal; catharsis; pity; fear; tragedy; plot

13.

...A perfect tragedy should, as we have seen, be arranged not on the simple but on the complex plan. It should, moreover, imitate actions which excite pity and fear, this being the distinctive mark of tragic imitation. It follows plainly, in the first place, that the change of fortune presented must not be the spectacle of a virtuous man brought from prosperity to adversity: for this moves neither pity nor fear; it merely shocks us. Not, again, of a bad man passing from adversity to prosperity: for nothing can be more alien to the spirit of Tragedy; it possesses no single tragic quality; it neither satisfies the moral sense nor calls forth pity or fear. Nor, again, should the downfall of the villain be exhibited. A plot of this kind would, doubtless, satisfy the moral sense, but it would inspire neither pity nor fear; for pity is aroused by unmerited misfortune, fear by the misfortune of a man like ourselves. Such an event, therefore, will be neither pitiful nor terrible. There remains, then, the character between these two extremes – that of a man who is not eminently good and just, yet whose misfortune is brought about not by vice or depravity, but by some error or frailty. He must be one who is highly renowned and prosperous – a personage like Oedipus, Thyestes, or other illustrious men of such families.

A well constructed plot should, therefore, be single in its issue, rather than double as some maintain. The change of fortune should be not from bad to good, but, reversely, from good to bad. It should come about as the result not of vice, but of some great error or frailty, in a character either such as we have described, or better rather than worse…

fortune; misfortune; plot; tragedy; action; pity; fear; morality; structure; audience/reader response; good and bad

14.

Actions capable of this effect must happen between persons who are either friends or enemies or indifferent to one another. If an enemy kills an enemy, there is nothing to excite pity either in the act or the intention – except so far as the suffering in itself is pitiful. So again with indifferent persons. But when the tragic accident occurs between those who are near or dear to one another – if, for example, a brother kills, or intends to kill, a brother, a son his father, a mother her son, a son his mother, or any other deed of the kind is done – these are the situations to be looked for by the poet. He may not indeed destroy the framework of the received legends...but he ought to show invention of his own, and skilfully handle the traditional material.

The action may be done consciously and with knowledge of the persons...Or, again, the deed of horror may be done, but done in ignorance, and the tie of kinship or friendship be discovered afterwards...Again, there is a third case – to be about to act with knowledge of the persons and then not to act. The fourth case is when someone is about to do an irreparable deed through ignorance, and makes the discovery before it is done. These are the only possible ways. For the deed must either be done or not done – and that wittingly or unwittingly. But of all these ways, to be about to act knowing the persons, and then not to act, is the worst. It is shocking without being tragic, for no disaster follows...The next and better way is that the deed should be perpetrated. Still better, that it should be perpetrated in ignorance, and the discovery made afterwards. There is then nothing to shock us, while the discovery produces a startling effect...

pleasure; intention; pity and fear; structure; plot; spectacle; action; character and relationships; morality

15.

In respect of Character there are four things to be aimed at. First, and most important, it must be good. Now any speech or action that manifests moral purpose of any kind will be expressive of character: the character will be good if the purpose is good. This rule is relative to each class. Even a woman may be good, and also a slave; though the woman may be said to be an inferior being, and the slave quite worthless. The second thing to aim at is propriety. There is a type of manly valour; but valour in a woman, or unscrupulous cleverness, is inappropriate. Thirdly, character must be true to life: for this is a distinct thing from goodness and propriety, as here described. The fourth point is consistency: for though the subject of the imitation, who suggested the type, be inconsistent, still he must be consistently inconsistent...

As in the structure of the plot, so too in the portraiture of character, the poet should always aim either at the necessary or the probable. Thus a person of given character should speak or act in a given way, by the rule either of necessity or of probability; just as this event should follow that by necessary or probable sequence. It is therefore evident that the unravelling of the plot, no less than the complication, must arise out of the plot itself, it must not be brought about by the *Deus ex Machina*...The *Deus ex Machina* should be employed only for events external to the drama – for antecedent or subsequent events, which lie beyond the range of human knowledge, and which require to be reported or foretold; for to the gods we ascribe the power of seeing all things. Within the action there must be nothing irrational. If the irrational cannot be excluded, it should be outside the scope of the tragedy...

character; moral purpose; class; gender; structure; necessity; probability; *Deus ex machina*; tragedy; imitation; true to life; rationality/irrationality

17.

In constructing the plot and working it out with the proper diction, the poet should place the scene, as far as possible, before his eyes. In this way, seeing everything with the utmost vividness, as if he were a spectator of the action, he will discover what is in keeping with it, and be most unlikely to overlook inconsistencies…

…As for the story, whether the poet takes it ready made or constructs it for himself, he should first sketch its general outline, and then fill in the episodes and amplify in detail…

After this, the names once given, it remains to fill in the episodes. We must see that they are relevant to the action…Thus the story of the Odyssey can be stated briefly. A certain man is absent from home for many years; he is jealously watched by Poseidon, and left desolate. Meanwhile, his home is in a wretched plight – suitors are wasting his substance and plotting against his son. At length, tempest-tost, he himself arrives; he makes certain persons acquainted with him; he attacks the suitors with his own hand, and is himself preserved while he destroys them. This is the essence of the plot; the rest is episode.

immediacy; emotion; life-like; synopsis; episode; plot; structure; imitation; cause and effect

18.

Every tragedy falls into two parts – Complication and Unravelling, or *Denouement*. Incidents extraneous to the action are frequently combined with a portion of the action proper, to form the Complication; the rest is the Unravelling. By the Complication I mean all that extends from the beginning of the action to the part which marks the turning-point to good or bad fortune. The Unravelling is that which extends from the beginning of the change to the end…

There are four kinds of Tragedy, the complex, depending entirely on Reversal of the Situation and Recognition; the Pathetic (where the motive is passion)…the Ethical (where the motives are ethical…The fourth kind is the Simple…The poet should endeavour, if possible, to combine all poetic elements; or failing that, the greatest number and those the most important; the more so, in face of the cavilling criticism of the day. For whereas there have hitherto been good poets, each in his own branch, the critics now expect one man to surpass all others in their several lines of excellence.

In speaking of a tragedy as the same or different, the best test to take is the plot. Identity exists where the Complication and Unravelling are the same. Many poets tie the knot well, but unravel it ill. Both arts, however, should always be mastered.

Again, the poet should remember what has been often said, and not make an Epic structure into a Tragedy – by an Epic structure I mean one with a multiplicity of plots – as if, for instance, you were to make a tragedy out of the entire story of the Iliad. In the Epic poem, owing to its length, each part assumes its proper magnitude. In the drama the result is far from answering to the poet's expectation…

complication; unravelling; denouement; structure; tragedy; epic; plot

19.

It remains to speak of Diction and Thought, the other parts of Tragedy having already been discussed. Concerning Thought, we may assume what is said in the Rhetoric, to which inquiry the subject more strictly belongs. Under Thought is included every effect which has to be produced by speech, the subdivisions being – proof and refutation; the excitation of the feelings, such as pity, fear, anger, and the like; the suggestion of importance or its opposite. Now, it is evident that the dramatic incidents must be treated from the same points of view as the dramatic speeches, when the object is to evoke the sense of pity, fear, importance or probability. The only difference is, that the incidents should speak for themselves without verbal exposition; while the effects aimed at in speech should be produced by the speaker, and as a result of the speech. For what were the business of a speaker, if the Thought were revealed quite apart from what he says?

Next, as regards Diction. One branch of the inquiry treats of the Modes of Utterance. But this province of knowledge belongs to the art of Delivery and to the masters of that science. It includes, for instance – what is a command, a prayer, a statement, a threat, a question, an answer and so forth. To know or not to know these things involves no serious censure upon the poet's art...

thought; diction; language; rhetoric; dialogue; performance; pity; fear; emotion; probability; subtext

25.

...The poet being an imitator, like a painter or any other artist, must of necessity imitate one of three objects – things as they were or are, things as they are said or thought to be, or things as they ought to be. The vehicle of expression is language – either current terms or, it may be, rare words or metaphors. There are also many modifications of language which we concede to the poets. Add to this, that the standard of correctness is not the same in poetry and politics, any more than in poetry and any other art. Within the art of poetry itself there are two kinds of faults – those which touch its essence and those which are accidental. If a poet has chosen to imitate something but has imitated it incorrectly through want of capacity, the error is inherent in the poetry. But if the failure is due to a wrong choice – if he has represented a horse as throwing out both his off legs at once, or introduced technical inaccuracies in medicine, for example, or in any other art – the error is not essential to the poetry...

First, as to matters which concern the poet's own art. If he describes the impossible, he is guilty of an error; but the error may be justified, if the end of the art be thereby attained... if, that is, the effect of this or any other part of the poem is rendered more striking...If, however, the end might have been as well, or better, attained without violating the special rules of the poetic art, the error is not justified: for every kind of error should, if possible be avoided...

Further, if it be objected that the description is not true to fact, the poet may perhaps reply – 'But the objects are as they ought to be'...If, however, the representation be of neither kind, the poet may answer – 'This is how men say the thing is.' This applies to tales about the gods...Again, a description may be no better than the fact: still, it was the fact...

In general, the impossible must be justified by reference to artistic requirements, or to the higher reality, or to received opinion. With respect to the requirements of art, a probable impossibility is to be preferred to a thing improbable and yet possible... 'Yes,' we say, 'but the impossible is the higher thing; for the ideal type must surpass the reality.' To justify the irrational, we appeal to what is commonly said to be. In addition to which, we urge that the irrational sometimes does not violate reason: just as 'it is probable that a thing may happen contrary to probability'.

truth; accuracy; description; purpose; ideal; function; intention; voyeuristic; criticism; language; possibility; probability; imitation; irrational; morality

RHETORIC (*335 BC*) (*translated by W. Rhys Roberts 1858-1929*).

Book One, Chapter 3

Rhetoric falls into three divisions, determined by the three classes of listeners to speeches. For of the three elements in speech-making – speaker, subject, and person addressed – it is the last one, the hearer that determines the speech's end and object.

speaker/author; subject/text; person addressed/reader; reader response; meaning

Chapter 4

...rhetoric is a combination of the science of logic and of the ethical branch of politics; and it is partly like dialectic, partly like sophistical reasoning. But the more we try to make either dialectic or rhetoric not what they really are, practical faculties, but sciences, the more we shall inadvertently be destroying their true nature; for we shall be re-fashioning them and shall be passing into the region of sciences dealing with definite subjects rather than simply with words and forms of reasoning...

Chapter 19

Let us first speak of the Possible and Impossible. It may plausibly be argued: That if it is possible for one pair of contraries to be or happen, then it is possible for the other: eg., if a man can be cured, he can also fall ill; for any two contraries are equally possible, in so far as they are contraries. That if of two similar things one is possible, so is the other. That if the harder of two things is possible, so is the easier. That if a thing can come into existence in a good and beautiful form, then it can come into existence generally; thus a house can exist more easily than a beautiful house. That if the beginning of a thing can occur, so can the end; for nothing impossible occurs or begins to occur... That if the end is possible, so is the beginning; for all things that occur have a beginning...That those things are possible of which the love or desire is natural; for no one, as a rule loves or desires impossibilities...That where the parts are possible, the whole is possible; and where the whole is possible, the parts are usually possible...That if a thing can be produced without art or preparation, it can be produced still more certainly by the careful application of art to it.

the possible; the impossible; logic; politics; dialectic; science; reasoning; contradiction; language; the scientific

Book Three, Chapter 2

...Style to be good must be clear, as is proved by the fact that speech which fails to convey a plain meaning will fail to do just what speech has to do. It must also be appropriate, avoiding both meanness and undue elevation; poetical language is certainly free from meanness, but it is not appropriate to prose. Clearness is secured by using the words (nouns and verbs alike) that are current and ordinary...People do not feel towards strangers as they do towards their own countrymen, and the same thing is true of their feeling for language. It is therefore well to give to everyday speech an unfamiliar air: people like what strikes them, and are struck by what is out of the way. In verse such effects are common, and there they are fitting: the persons and things there spoken of are comparatively remote from ordinary life. In prose passages they are far less often fitting because the subject-matter is less exalted. Even in poetry, it is not quite appropriate that fine language should be used by a slave or a very young man, or about very trivial subjects: even in poetry the style, to be appropriate, must sometimes be toned down, though at other times heightened. We can now see that a writer must disguise his art and give the impression of speaking naturally and not artificially.

…metaphor is of great value both in poetry and prose. Prose-writers must, however, pay specially careful attention to metaphor, because their other resources are scantier than those of poets. Metaphor, moreover, gives style clearness, charm, and distinction as nothing else can: and it is not a thing whose use can be taught by one man to another. Metaphors, like epithets, must be fitting, which means that they must fairly correspond to the thing signified: failing this, their inappropriateness will be conspicuous: the want of harmony between two things is emphasised by their being placed side by side. It is like having to ask ourselves what dress will suit an old man; certainly not the crimson cloak that suits a young man…Further, in using metaphors to give names to nameless things, we must draw them not from remote but from kindred and similar things, so that the kinship is clearly perceived as soon as the words are said…The materials of metaphor must be beautiful to the ear, to the understanding, to the eye or some other physical sense…

prose; poetry; register; metaphor; clarity; style; meaning; the vernacular

Chapter 7

Your language will be *appropriate* if it expresses emotion and character, and if it corresponds to its subject... To express emotion, you will employ the language of anger in speaking of outrage; the language of disgust and discreet reluctance to utter a word when speaking of impiety or foulness; the language of exultation for a tale of glory, and that of humiliation for a tale of pity...

This aptness of language is one thing that makes people believe in the truth of your story: their minds draw the false conclusion that you are to be trusted from the fact that others behave as you do when things are as you describe them; and therefore they take your story to be true, whether it is so or not. Besides, an emotional speaker always makes his audience feel with him, even when there is nothing in his arguments: which is why many speakers try to overwhelm their audience by mere noise.

register; convincing; empathy; emotion; character; vocabulary; aptness; reader response

Chapter 13

A speech has two parts. You must state your case, and you must prove it. You cannot either state your case and omit to prove it, or prove it without having first stated it; since any proof must be a proof of something, and the only use of a preliminary statement is the proof that follows it. Of these two parts the first part is called the Statement of the case, the second part the Argument, just as we distinguish between Enunciation and Demonstration...It follows, then, that the only necessary parts of a speech are the Statement and the Argument. These are the essential features of a speech; and it cannot in any case have more than Introduction, Statement, Argument, and Epilogue. 'Refutation of the Opponent' is part of the arguments; so is 'Comparison' of the opponent's case with your own, for that process is a magnifying of your own case and therefore a part of the arguments, since one who does this *proves* something. The Introduction does nothing like this; nor does the Epilogue – it merely reminds us of what has been said already...

Chapter 14

The Introduction is the beginning of a speech, corresponding to the prologue in poetry and the prelude in flute-music; they are all beginnings, paving the way, as it were, for what is to follow. The musical prelude resembles the introduction to speeches of display; as flute-players play first some brilliant passages they know well and then fit it on to the opening notes of the piece itself, so in speeches of display the writer should proceed in the same way; he should begin with what best takes his fancy, and then strike up his theme and lead into it; which is indeed what *is* always done.

argument; proof; statement; enunciation; demonstration; structure

HORACE (65–8 BC)

THE ART OF POETRY *(c. 15 BC) (translated into English verse by John Conington 1825-1869)*

Suppose some painter, as a tour de force,
Should couple head of man with neck of horse,
Invest them both with feathers, 'stead of hair,
And tack on limbs picked up from here to there,
So that the figure, when complete, should show
A maid above, a hideous fish below:
Should you be favoured with a private view,
You'd laugh, my friends, I know, and rightly too.
Yet trust me, Pisos, not less strange would look,
To a discerning eye, the foolish book
Where dream-like forms in sick delirium blend,
And nought is of a piece from end to end.
'Poets and painters (sure you know the plea)
have always been allowed their fancy free.'
I own it; tis a fair excuse to plead;
By turns we claim it and by turns concede;
But 'twill not screen the unnatural and absurd,
Unions of lamb with tiger, snake with bird.

imitation; incongruity; imagination; unconscious; accuracy

…we poor sons of song
Oft find 'tis fancied right that leads us wrong.
I prove obscure in trying to be terse;
Attempts at ease emasculate my verse;
Who aims at grandeur into bombast falls;
Who fears to stretch his pinions creeps and crawls;
Who hopes by strange variety to please
Puts dolphins among forests, boars in seas.
Thus zeal to 'scape from error, if unchecked
By sense of art, creates a new defect.
Fix on some casual sculptor; he shall know
How to give nails their sharpness, hair its flow;
Yet he shall fail, because he lacks the soul
To comprehend and reproduce the whole.
I'd not be he; the blackest hair and eye
Lose all their beauty with the nose awry.

accessibility; imitation; verisimilitude; gender; realism

Good authors, take a brother bard's advice:
Ponder your subject o'er not once nor twice,
And oft and oft consider, if the weight
You hope to lift be or be not too great.
Let but our theme be equal to our powers,
Choice language, clear arrangement, both are ours.
Would you be told how best your pearls to thread?
Why, say just now what should just now be said,
But put off other matter for today,
To introduce it later by the way.

In words again be cautious and select,
And duly pick out this, and that reject.
High praise and honour to the bard is due
Whose dexterous setting makes an old word new.
Nay more, should some recondite subject need
Fresh signs to make it clear to those who read,
A power of issuing terms till now unused,
If claimed with modesty, is ne'er refused.
New words will find acceptance, if they flow
Forth from the Greek, with just a twist or so.

thought; imitation; structure; language; selection; originality

Unless the speaker's words and fortune suit,
All Rome will join to jeer him, horse and foot.
Gods should not talk like heroes, nor again
Impetuous youth like grave and reverend men;
Lady and nurse a different language crave,
Sons of the soil and rovers o'er the wave;
Assyrian, Colchian, Theban, Argive, each
Has his own style, his proper cast of speech.

In painting characters, adhere to fame,
Or study keeping in the type you frame:
If great Achilles figure in the scene,
Make him impatient, fiery, ruthless, keen;
All laws, all covenants let him still disown,
And test his quarrel by the sword alone.
Still be Medea all revenge and scorn,
Ino still sad, Ixion still forsworn,
Io a wanderer still, Orestes still forlorn.

If you would be original, and seek
To frame some character ne'er seen in Greek,
See it be wrought on one consistent plan,
And end the same creation it began.
'Tis hard, I grant, to treat a subject known
And hackneyed so that it may look one's own;
Far better turn the Iliad to a play
And carve out acts and scenes the readiest way,
Than alter facts and characters, and tell
In a strange form the tale men know so well.

conventions; genre; audience; history; research; character; types; stereotypes; register; verisimilitude

Sometimes an action on the stage is shown,
Sometimes 'tis done elsewhere, and there made known.
A thing when heard, remember, strikes less keen
On the spectator's mind than when 'tis seen.
Yet 'twere not well in public to display
A business best transacted far away,
And much may be secluded from the eye
For well-graced tongues to tell of by and by.
Medea must not shed her children's blood,
Nor savage Atreus cook man's flesh for food…
If scenes like these before my eyes be thrust,
They shock belief and generate disgust.

show/tell; reported speech; dialogue; action; morality; censorship

The Iambic foot is briefly thus defined:
Two syllables, a short with long behind:
Repeat it six times o'er, so quick its beat,
'Tis trimester, three measures for six feet:
At first it ran straight on; but years ago,
Its hearers begged that it would move more slow;
On which it took, with a good-natured air,
Stout spondees in, its native rights to share,
Yet so that none should ask it to resign
The sixth, fourth, second places in the line.

What shall a poet do? Make rules his sport,
And dash through thick and thin, through long and short?
Or pick his steps, endeavour to walk clean,
And fancy every mud-stain will be seen?
What good were that, if though I mind my ways
And shun all blame, I do not merit praise.
My friends, make Greece your model when you write,
And turn her volumes over day and night.

poetry; metre; iambic foot; imitation; reading; intertextual

Of writing well, be sure, the secret lies
In wisdom: therefore study to be wise.
The page of Plato may suggest the thought,
Which found, the words will come as soon as sought.
The man who once has learned to comprehend
His duty to his country and his friend,
The love that parent, brother, guest may claim.
The judge's, senator's, or general's aim,
That man, when need occurs, will soon invent

For every part its proper sentiment.
Look too to life and manners as they lie
Before you: these will living words supply.
A play, devoid of beauty, strength and art,
So but the thoughts and morals suit each part,
Will catch men's minds and rivet them when caught
More than the clink of verses without thought.

knowledge; subject matter; historical precedence; imitation; write what you know; technique; morality; research; study/learning; thinking

LONGINUS
(ascribed to, fl. 1st century AD)

***

ON THE SUBLIME *(translated by. H. L. Havell)*

1.

I am addressing a person so accomplished in literature, I need only state, without enlarging further on the matter, that the Sublime, wherever it occurs, consists in a certain loftiness and excellence of language, and that it is by this, and this only, that the greatest poets and prose-writers have gained eminence, and won themselves a lasting place in the Temple of Fame...

A lofty passage does not convince the reason of the reader, but takes him out of himself. That which is admirable ever confounds our judgement, and eclipses that which is merely reasonable or agreeable. To believe or not is usually in our own power; but the Sublime, acting with an imperious and irresistible force, sways every reader whether he will or no. Skill in invention, lucid arrangement and disposition of facts, are appreciated not by one passage or two, but gradually manifest themselves in the general structure of a work; but a sublime thought, if happily timed, illumines an entire subject with the vividness of a lightning-flash, and exhibits the whole power of the orator in a moment of time.

value judgement; rhetoric; style; expression; escapism; sublime; reading; audience; performance; passion; structure; craft; aesthetics; language; beauty

2.

The first question which presents itself for solution is whether there is any art which can teach sublimity or loftiness in writing. For some hold generally that there is mere delusion in attempting to reduce such subjects to technical rules. 'The Sublime,' they tell us, ' is born in a man, and not to be acquired by instruction; genius is the only master who can teach it...'

...Nature in her loftier and more passionate moods, while detesting all appearance of restraint, is not wont to show herself utterly wayward and reckless; and though in all cases the vital informing principle is derived from her, yet to determine the right degree and the right moment, is the peculiar province of scientific method. The great passions, when left to their own blind and rash impulses without the control of reason, are in the same danger as a ship let drive at random without ballast.

pedagogy; craft; genius; reason/passion; gender; science; talent

10.

Let us now consider whether there is anything further which conduces to the Sublime in writing. It is a law of Nature that in all things there are certain constituent parts, coexistent with their substance. It necessarily follows, therefore, that one cause of sublimity is the choice of the most striking circumstances involved in whatever we are describing, and, further, the power of afterwards combining them into one animate whole. The reader is attracted partly by the selection of incidents, partly by the skill which has welded them together. For instance, Sappho, in dealing with the passionate manifestations attending on the frenzy of lovers, always chooses her strokes from the signs which she has observed to be actually exhibited in such cases. But her peculiar excellence lies in the felicity with which she chooses and unites together the most striking and powerful features.

selection; structure; order; narrative; passion

13.

…there is yet another path besides those mentioned which leads to sublime heights. What path do I mean? The emulous imitation of the great poets and prose-writers of the past… Many gather the divine impulse from another's spirit, just as we are told that the Pythian priestess, when she takes her seat on the tripod, where there is said to be a rent in the ground breathing upwards a heavenly emanation, straightway conceives from that source the godlike gift of prophecy, and utters her inspired oracles; so likewise from the mighty genius of the great writers of antiquity there is carried into the souls of their rivals, as from a fount of inspiration, an effluence which breathes upon them until, even though their natural temper be but cold, they share the sublime enthusiasm of others…

Now what I am speaking of is not plagiarism, but resembles the process of copying from fair forms or statues or works of skilled labour. Nor in my opinion would so many fair flowers of imagery have bloomed among the philosophical domains of Plato, nor would he have risen so often to the language and topics of poetry, had he not engaged heart and soul in a contest for precedence with Homer, like a young champion entering the lists against a veteran...

intertextuality; sensibility; tradition; imitation; reading; inspiration; plagiarism; pedagogy; competition

15.

...Poets and orators both employ images, but with a very different object, as you are well aware. The poetical image is designed to astound; the oratorical image to give perspicuity. Both, however, seek to work on the emotions...

...in poetry...a certain mythical exaggeration is allowable, transcending altogether mere logical credence. But the chief beauties of an oratorical image are its energy and reality. Such digressions become offensive and monstrous when the language is cast in a poetical and fabulous mould, and runs into all sorts of impossibilities...

Wherein, then, lies the force of an oratorical image? Doubtless in adding energy and passion in a hundred different ways to a speech; but especially in this, that when it is mingled with the practical, argumentative parts of an oration, it does not merely convince the hearer but enthrals him...

In all such cases our nature is drawn towards that which affects it most powerfully: hence an image lures us away from an argument: judgement is paralysed, matters of fact disappear from view, eclipsed by the superior blaze. Nor is it surprising that we should be thus affected; for when two forces are thus placed in juxtaposition, the stronger must always absorb itself into the weaker.

image; idea; passion; audience; evocation; illusion; suspension of disbelief; imaginative; discursive; oratory; rhetoric; clarity; emotions; general/concrete; conviction; absorption; reader; argument/emotion; rational/irrational

25.

When past events are introduced as happening in present time the narrative form is changed into a dramatic action.

27.

Sometimes, again, a writer in the midst of a narrative in the third person suddenly steps aside and makes a transition to the first. It is a kind of figure which strikes like a sudden outburst of passion.

style; reality; gender; dialogue; passions; non-sequitur; imitation; narration; prose; drama; action; dialogue; narration; first/third person; point of view

PLOTINUS *(3rd century AD)*

AN ESSAY ON THE BEAUTIFUL (*translated by Thomas Taylor 1758–1835*)

Beauty for the most part, consists in objects of sight; but it is also received through the ears, by the skilful composition of words, and the consonant proportion of sounds; for in every species of harmony, beauty is to be found. And if we rise from sense into the regions of soul, we shall there perceive studies and offices, actions and habits, sciences and virtues, invested with a much larger portion of beauty. But whether there is above these, a still higher beauty, will appear as we advance in its investigation. What is it then, which causes bodies to appear fair to the sight, sounds beautiful to the ear, and science and virtue lovely to the mind? Whether beauty is one and the same in all? Or, whether the beauty of bodies is of one kind, and the beauty of souls is another? And again, what these are, if they are two? Or, what beauty is, if perfectly simple, and one? For some things, as bodies, are doubtless beautiful, not from the natures of the subjects in which they reside, but rather by some kind of participation; but others again appear to be essentially beautiful, or beauties themselves; and such is the nature of virtue. For, with respect, to the same bodies, they appear beautiful to one person, and the reverse of beauty to another; as if the essence of body were a thing different from the essence of beauty. In the first place then, what is that, which by its presence, causes the beauty of bodies? Let us reflect, what most powerfully attracts the eyes of beholders, and seizes the spectator with rapturous delight; for if we can find what this is, we may perhaps use it as a ladder, enabling us to ascend into the region of beauty, and survey its immeasurable extent.

It is the general opinion that a certain commensuration of parts to each other, and to the whole, with the addition, of colour, generates that beauty which is the object of sight; and that in the commensurate and the moderate alone the beauty of everything consists. But from such an opinion the compound only, and not the simple, can be beautiful, the single parts will have no peculiar beauty; and will only merit that appellation by conferring to the beauty of the whole. But it is surely necessary that a lovely whole should consist of beautiful parts, for the fair can never rise out of the deformed. But from such a definition, it follows, that beautiful colours and the light of the sun, since they are simple and do not receive their beauty from commensuration, must be excluded the regions of beauty. Besides, how, from such a hypothesis can gold be beautiful? Or the glittering of night and the glorious spectacle of the stars? In like manner, the most simple musical sounds will be foreign from beauty, though in a song wholly beautiful every note must be beautiful as necessary to the being of the whole. Again, since the same proportion remaining, and the same face is to one person beautiful and to another the reverse, is it not necessary to call the beauty of the commensurate one kind of beauty and the commensuration another kind, and that the commensurate is fair by means of something else?

But if transferring themselves to beautiful studies and fair discourses, they shall assign as the cause of beauty in these the proportion of measure, what is that which in beautiful sciences, laws of disciplines, is called commensurate proportion? Or in what manner can speculations themselves be called mutually commensurate? If it be said because of the inherent concord, we reply that there is a certain concord and consent in evil souls, a conformity of sentiment, in believing (as it is said) that temperance is folly and justice a generous ignorance. It appears, therefore, that the beauty of the soul is every virtue, and this species of the beautiful possessed far greater reality than any of the superior we have mentioned. But after what manner in this is commensuration to be found? For it is neither like the symmetry in magnitude nor in numbers. And since the parts of the soul are many, in what proportion and synthesis, in what temperament of parts or concord of speculations, does beauty consist? Lastly, of what kind is the beauty of intellect itself, abstracted from every corporeal concern, and intimately conversing with itself alone?

beauty; aesthetics; structure; language; soul; audience; intellect; emotion; point of view

PART TWO

*Sixteenth-Seventeenth
Centuries*

MICHEL DE MONTAIGNE
(1533–1592)

Of the Force of Imagination *(1580)*

I am one of those who are most sensible of the power of
imagination: every one is jostled by it, but some are overthrown
by it. It has a very piercing impression upon me; and I make
it my business to avoid, wanting force to resist it. I could live
by the sole help of healthful and jolly company; the very sight
of another's pain materially pains me, and I often usurp the
sensations of another person. A perpetual cough in another
tickles my lungs and throat. I more unwillingly visit the sick in
whom by love and duty I am interested, than those I care not
for, to whom I less look. I take possession of the disease I am
concerned at, and take it to myself. I do not at all wonder that
fancy should give fevers and sometimes kill such as allow it too
much scope and are too willing to entertain it...

I myself knew a gentleman, who having treated a large
company at his house, three or four days after bragged in jest
(for there was no such thing), that he had made them eat of a
baked cat; at which, a young gentlewoman, who had been at
the feast, took such a horror, that falling into a violent vomiting
and fever, there was no possible means to save her. Even brute

beasts are subject to the force of imagination as well as we; witness dogs, who die of grief for the loss of their masters; and bark and tremble and start in their sleep…

Now all this may be attributed to the close affinity and relation betwixt the soul and the body intercommunicating their fortunes; but 'tis quite another thing when the imagination works not only upon one's own particular body, but upon that of others also. And as an infected body communicates its malady to those that approach or live near it, as we see in the plague, the smallpox, and sore eyes, that run through whole families and cities…so the imagination, being vehemently agitated, darts out infection capable of offending the foreign object. The ancients had an opinion of certain women of Scythia, that being animated and enraged against any one, they killed him only with their looks. Tortoises and ostriches hatch their eggs with only looking on them, which infers that their eyes have in them some ejaculative virtue…

I am solicited to write the affairs of my own time by some, who fancy I look upon them with an eye less blinded with passion than another, and have a clearer insight into them by reason of the free access fortune has given me to the heads of various factions; but they do not consider, that to purchase the glory of Sallust, I would not give myself the trouble, sworn enemy as I am to obligation, assiduity or perseverance: that there is nothing so contrary to my style, as a continued narrative, I so often interrupt and cut myself short in my writing for want of breath; I have neither composition nor explanation worth anything, and am ignorant, beyond a child, of the phrases and even the very words proper to express the most common things; and for that reason it is, that I have undertaken to say only what I can say, and have accommodated my subject to my strength.

imagination; sympathy; empathy; fancy; history; body; soul;
fiction; narrative; spontaneity; body, soul; gender; realism;
passion; style

GEORGE PUTTENHAM
(–1590)

THE ARTE OF ENGLISH POESIE *(1589) (in the original spelling)*

Chapter 4

How the Poets were the first Philosophers, the first Astronomers and Historiographers and Oratours and Musiciens of the world.

Vtterance also and language is giuen by nature to man for perswasion of others, and aide of them selues, I meane the first abilite to speake. For speech it selfe is artificiall and made by man, and the more pleasing it is, the more it preuaileth to such purpose as it is intended for: but speech by meeter is a kind of vtterance, more cleanly couched and more delicate to the eare then prose is, because it is more currant and slipper vpon the tongue, and withal tunable and melodious, as a kind of Musicke, and therfore may be tearmed a musicall speech or vtterance, which cannot but please the hearer very well. Another cause is, for that it is briefer & more compendious, and easier to beare away and be retained in memorie, then that which is contained in multitude of words and full of tedious ambage and long periods. It is beside a maner of vtterance more eloquent and rethoricall then the ordinarie prose, which we use in our daily talke: because it is decked and set out with all manner of fresh colours and figures, which maketh that it sooner inuegleth the iudgement of man, and carieth his opinion this way and that, whither soeuer the heart by impression of the eare shal be most affectionatly bent and directed. The vtterance in prose is not of so great efficacie, because not only it is dayly vsed, and by that occasion the eare is ouerglutted with it, but is also not so voluble and slipper vpon the tong, being wide and lose, and nothing numerous, nor contriued into measures, and sounded with so gallant and harmonical accents, nor in fine alowed that figuratiue conueyance, nor so great licence in choise of words and phrases as meeter is. So as the Poets were also from the beginning the best perswaders and their eloquence the first Rethoricke of the world. Euen so it became that the high mysteries of the gods should be reuealed & taught, by a maner of vtterance and language of extraordinarie phrase, and briefe and compendious, and aboue al others sweet and ciuill as the Metricall is. The same also was meetest to register the liues and noble gests of Princes, and of the great Monarkes of the world, and all other the memorable accidents of time: so as the Poet was also the first historiographer. Then for as much as they were the first obseruers of all naturall causes & effects in the things generable and corruptible, and from thence mounted vp to search after the celestiall courses and influences, & yet penetrated further to know the diuine essences and substances separate, as is sayd before, they were the first Astronomers and Philosophists and Metaphisicks. Finally, because they did altogether endeuor themselues to reduce the life of man to a certaine method of good maners, and made the first differences betweene vertue and vice, and then tempered all these knowledges and skilles with the exercise of a delectable Musicke by melodious instruments, which withall serued them to delight their hearers, & to call the people together by admiration, to a plausible and vertuous conuersation, therefore were they the first Philosophers Ethick, & the first artificial Musiciens of the world.

rhetoric; superiority of poets; historians; musicians; philosophers; poetry; prose

Book Three, Chapter Five, Of Stile

Stile is a constant & continuall phrase or tenour of speaking and writing, extending to the whole tale or processe of the poeme or historie, and not properly to any peece or member of a tale: but is of words speeches and sentences together, a certaine contriued forme and qualitie, many times naturall to the writer, many times his peculier by election and arte, and such as either he keepeth by skill, or holdeth on by ignorance, and will not or peraduenture cannot easily alter into any other...And because this continuall course and manner of writing or speech sheweth the matter and disposition of the writers minde, more than one or few words or sentences can shew, therefore there be that haue called stile, the image of man *mentes character* for man is but his minde, and as his minde is tempered and qualified, so are his speeches and language at large, and his inward conceits be the mettall of his minde and his manner of vtterance the very warp & woofe of his conceits, more plaine, or busie and intricate, or otherwise affected after the rate...For if the man be graue, his speech and stile is graue: if light-headed, his stile and language also light: if the minde be haughtie and hoate, the speech and stile is also vehement and stirring: if it be colde and temperate, the stile is also very modest: if it be humble, or base and meeke, so is also the language and stile…Then againe may it be said as wel, that men doo chuse their subjects according to the mettal of their minds, & therfore a high minded man chuseth him high & lofty matter to write of.

style; subject matter; high and low art

SIR PHILIP SIDNEY
(1554–1586)

AN APOLOGIE FOR POETRIE/
THE DEFENCE OF POESIE *(1581)*

…I know not by what mischance, in these my not old years and idlest times, having slipped into the title of a poet, am provoked to say something unto you in the defence of that my unelected vocation; which if I handle with more good will than good reasons, bear with me…

Among the Romans a poet was called 'vates', which is as much as a diviner, foreseer, or prophet…so heavenly a title did that excellent people bestow upon this heart-ravishing knowledge!

…But now let us see how the Greeks have named it, and how they deemed of it. The Greeks named him poet, which name hath, as the most excellent, gone through other languages…wherein, I know not whether by luck or wisdom, we Englishmen have met with the Greeks in calling him a 'maker', which name, how high and incomparable it is, I had rather were known by marking the scope of other sciences, than by any partial allegation. There is no art delivered unto mankind that hath not the works of nature for his principal object, without which they could not consist, and on which they so depend, as they become actors and players, as it were, of what nature will have set forth…Only the poet, disdaining to be tied to any such subjection, lifted up with the vigour of his own invention, doth grow, in effect, into another nature; in making things either better than nature bringeth forth, or quite anew; forms such as never were in nature, as the heroes, demi-gods, Cyclops, chimeras, furies, and such like; so as he goeth hand in hand with Nature, not enclosed within the narrow warrant of her gifts, but freely ranging within the zodiac of his own wit. Nature never set forth the earth in so rich tapestry as divers poets have done; neither with so pleasant rivers, fruitful trees, sweet-smelling flowers, nor whatsoever else may make the too-loved earth more lovely; her world is brazen, the poets only deliver a golden.

…Poesy, therefore, is an art of imitation; for so Aristotle termed it…that is to say, a representing, counterfeiting or figuring forth: to speak metaphorically, a speaking picture, with this end, to teach and delight.

Of this have been three general kinds: the CHIEF, both in antiquity and excellency, which they that did imitate the inconceivable excellencies of God…The SECOND kind is of them that deal with matter philosophical…the THIRD, indeed right poets…For these, indeed, do merely make to imitate, and imitate both to delight and teach, and delight to move men to take that goodness in hand, which, without delight they would fly as from a stranger; and teach to make them know that goodness whereunto they are moved; which being the noblest scope to which ever any learning was directed, yet want there not idle tongues to bark at them…

…So that the ending end of all earthly learning being

virtuous action, those skills that most serve to bring forth that have a most just title to be princes over all the rest; wherein, if we can show it rightly, the poet is worthy to have it before any other competitors.

...The philosopher, therefore, and the historian are they which would win the goal, the one by precept, the other by example; but not having both, do both halt. For the philosopher, setting down with thorny arguments the bare rule, is so hard of utterance, and so misty to be conceived, that one that hath no other guide but him shall wade in him until he be old, before he shall find sufficient cause to be honest. For his knowledge standeth so upon the abstract and general, that happy is the man who may understand him, and more happy that can apply what he doth understand. On the other side, the historian, wanting the precept, is so tied, not to what should be, but to what is; to the particular truth of things, and not to the general reason of things; that his example draweth no necessary consequence, and therefore a less fruitful doctrine.

Now doth the peerless poet perform both; for whatsoever the philosopher saith should be done, he giveth a perfect picture of it, by some one by whom he presupposeth it was done, so as he coupleth the general notion with the particular example. A perfect picture, I say; for he yieldeth to the powers of the mind an image of that whereof the philsopopher bestoweth but a wordish description, which doth neither strike, pierce, nor possess the sight of the soul, so much as that other doth. For, as in outward things, to a man that had never seen an elephant, or a rhinoceros, who should tell him most exquisitely all their shape, colour, bigness and particular marks? Or of a gorgeous palace, an architect, who, declaring the full beauties, might well make the hearer able to repeat, as it were, by rote, all he had heard, yet should never satisfy his inward conceit, with being witness to itself of a true living knowledge; but the same man, as soon as he might see those beasts well painted, or that house well in model, should straightway grow, without need of any description, to a judicial comprehending of them; so, no doubt, the philosopher, with his learned definitions, be it of virtue or vices, matters of public policy or private government, replenisheth the memory with many infallible grounds of wisdom, which, notwithstanding, lie dark before the imaginative and judging power, if they be not illuminated or figured forth by the speaking picture of poesy...

But now it may be alleged, that if thus managing of matters be so fit for the imagination, then must the historian needs surpass, who brings you images of true matters, such as, indeed, were done, and not such as fantastically or falsely may be suggested to have been done...And whereas, a man may say, in universal consideration of doctrine, the poet prevaileth, yet that the history, in his saying such a thing was done, doth warrant a man more in that he shall follow; the answer is manifest: that if he stand upon that WAS, as if he should argue, because it rained yesterday therefore it should rain today; then, indeed, hath it some advantage to a gross conceit. But if he know an example only enforms a conjectured likelihood, and so go by reason, the poet doth so far exceed him, as he is to frame his example to that which is most reasonable, be it in warlike, politic or private matters; where the historian in his bare WAS hath many times that which we call fortune to overrule the best wisdom. Many times he must tell events whereof he can yield no cause; or if he do, it must be poetically.

For, that a feigned example hath as much force to teach as a true example (for as for to move, it is clear, since the feigned may be tuned to the highest key of passion)…So, then, the best of the historians is subject to the poet; for, whatsoever action or faction, whatsoever counsel, policy or war stratagem the historian is bound to recite, that may the poet, if he list, with his imitation, make his own, beautifying it both for farther teaching, and more delighting, as it please him: having all, from Dante's heaven to his hell, under the authority of his pen…

Now, therein, of all sciences (I speak still of human and according to the human conceit), is our poet the monarch. For he doth not only show the way, but giveth so sweet a prospect into the way, as will entice any man to enter into it; nay, he doth, as if your journey should lie through a fair vineyard, at the very first give you a cluster of grapes, that full of that taste you may long to pass farther. He beginneth not with obscure definitions, which must blur the margin with interpretations, and load the memory with doubtfulness, but he cometh to you with words set in delightful proportion, either accompanied with, or prepared for, the well-enchanting skill of music; and with a tale, forsooth, he cometh unto you with a tale which holdeth children from play, and old men from the chimney-corner; and, pretending no more, doth intend the winning of the mind from wickedness to virtue; even as the child is often brought to take most wholesome things, by hiding them in such other as have a pleasant taste; which, if one should begin to tell them the nature of the aloes or rhubarbarum they should receive, would sooner take their physic at their ears than at their mouth; so it is in men (most of them are childish in the best things, till they be cradled in their graves)…

Since, then, poetry is of all human learnings the most ancient, and of most fatherly antiquity, as from whence other learnings have taken their beginnings; since it is so universal that no learned nation doth despise it, nor barbarous nation is without it; since both Roman and Greek gave such divine names unto it, the one of prophesying, the other of making, and that indeed that name of making is fit for him, considering, that where all other arts retain themselves within their subject, and receive, as it were, their being from it, the poet only, only bringeth his own stuff, and doth not learn a conceit out of a matter, but maketh matter for a conceit; since neither his description nor his end containeth any evil, the thing described cannot be evil; since his effects be so good as to teach goodness, and delight the learners of it; since therein (namely, in moral doctrine, the chief of all knowledges) he doth not only far pass the historian, but, for instruction, is well nigh comparable to the philosopher; for moving, leaveth behind him; since the Holy Scriptures (wherein there is no uncleanness) hath whole parts in it poetical, and that even our Saviour Christ vouchsafed to use the flowers of it; since all his kinds are not only in their united forms, but in their severed dissections fully commendable; I think, and think I think rightly, the laurel crown appointed for triumphant captains, doth worthily, of all other learnings, honour the poet's triumph...

poet as maker; prophet; maker; imitation; imagination; philosophy; morality; argument; history/historian; research; philosophy/philosopher; poet as superior to historian and philosopher; knowledge; the general; the particular; soul; probability; teaching/learning; desire; passion; intention; lying; inspiration; the Muses

FRANCIS BACON (1561–1626)

THE ADVANCEMENT OF LEARNING
(*1605*)

The parts of human learning have reference to the three parts of man's understanding, which is the seat of learning: history to his memory, poesy to his imagination, and philosophy to his reason. Divine learning receiveth the same distribution; for, the spirit of man is the same, though the revelation of oracle and sense be diverse. So as theology consisteth also of history of the Church; of parables, which is divine poesy; and of holy doctrine or precept. For as for that part which seemeth supernumerary, which is prophecy, it is but divine history, which hath that prerogative over human, as the narration may be before the fact as well as after.

Poesy is a part of learning in measure of words, for the most part restrained, but in all other points extremely licensed, and doth truly refer to the imagination; which, being not tied to the laws of matter, may at pleasure join that which nature hath severed, and sever that which nature hath joined, and so make unlawful matches and divorces of things--Pictoribus atque poetis, &c. It is taken in two senses in respect of words or matter. In the first sense, it is but a character of style, and belongeth to arts of speech, and is not pertinent for the present. In the latter, it is--as hath been said--one of the principal portions of learning, and is nothing else but feigned history, which may be styled as well in prose as in verse.

...because the acts or events of true history have not that magnitude which satisfieth the mind of man, poesy feigneth acts and events greater and more heroical. Because true history propoundeth the successes and issues of actions not so agreeable to the merits of virtue and vice, therefore poesy feigns them more just in retribution, and more according to revealed Providence. Because true history representeth actions and events more ordinary and less interchanged, therefore poesy endureth them with more rareness and more unexpected and alternative variations. So as it appeareth that poesy serveth and conferreth to magnanimity, morality and to delectation. And therefore, it was ever thought to have some participation of divineness, because it doth raise and erect the mind, by submitting the shows of things to the desires of the mind; whereas reason doth buckle and bow the mind unto the nature of things.

The division of poesy which is aptest in the propriety thereof (besides those divisions which are common unto it with history, as feigned chronicles, feigned lives, and the appendices of history, as feigned epistles, feigned orations, and the rest) is into poesy narrative, representative, and allusive. The narrative is a mere imitation of history, with the excesses before remembered, choosing for subjects commonly wars and love, rarely state, and sometimes pleasure or mirth. Representative is as a visible history, and is an image of actions as if they were present, as history is of actions in nature as they are (that is) past. Allusive, or parabolical, is a narration applied only to express some special purpose or conceit; which latter kind of parabolical wisdom was much more in use in the ancient times, as by the fables of AEsop, and the brief sentences of the seven, and the use of hieroglyphics may appear.

...Neither is the imagination simply and only a messenger; but is invested with, or at least wise usurpeth no small authority in itself, besides the duty of the message. For it was well said by Aristotle, 'That the mind hath over the body that commandment, which the lord hath over a bondman; but that reason hath over the imagination that commandment which a magistrate hath over a free citizen,' who may come also to rule in his turn. For we see that, in matters of faith and religion, we raise our imagination above our reason, which is the cause why religion sought ever access to the mind by similitudes, types, parables, visions, dreams. And again, in all persuasions that are wrought by eloquence, and other impressions of like nature, which do paint and disguise the true appearance of things, the chief recommendation unto reason is from the imagination. Nevertheless, because I find not any science that doth properly or fitly pertain to the imagination, I see no cause to alter the former division. For as for poesy, it is rather a pleasure or play of imagination than a work or duty thereof. And if it be a work, we speak not now of such parts of learning as the imagination produceth, but of such sciences as handle and consider of the imagination.

...Notwithstanding, to stir the earth a little about the roots of this science, as we have done of the rest, the duty and office of rhetoric is to apply reason to imagination for the better moving of the will...For the end of logic is to teach a form of argument to secure reason, and not to entrap it; the end of morality is to procure the affections to obey reason, and not to invade it; the end of rhetoric is to fill the imagination to second reason, and not to oppress it; for these abuses of arts come in but ex oblique, for caution.

style; knowledge; history; poetry; philosophy; imagination; truth; narrative; reason; pleasure; science; rhetoric; logic; science; religion

WILLIAM SHAKESPEARE (1564–1616)

A MIDSUMMER NIGHT'S DREAM *(Act V, Sc. 1)*

THESEUS:
The lunatic, the lover and the poet
Are of imagination all compact:
One sees more devils than vast hell can hold –
That is the madman: the lover, all as frantic,
Sees Helen's beauty in a brow of Egypt:
The poet's eye, in a fine frenzy rolling,
Doth glance from heaven to earth, from earth to heaven;
And as imagination bodies forth
The forms of things unknown, the poet's pen
Turns them to shapes and gives to airy nothing
A local habitation and a name.
Such tricks hath strong imagination,
That if it would but apprehend some joy,
It comprehends some bringer of that joy;
Or in the night, imagining some fear,
How easy is a bush supposed a bear!

inspiration; lying; imagination

BEN JONSON (1573–1637)

TIMBER, DISCOVERIES MADE UPON MEN AND MATTER *(1641)*

Scientiae liberalis. – Arts that respect the mind were ever reputed nobler than those of the body, though we less can be without them, as tillage, spinnage, weaving, building, &c., without which we could scarce sustain life a day. But these were the works of every hand; the other of the brain only, and those the most generous and exalted wits and spirits, that cannot rest or acquiesce. The mind of man is still fed with labour...

writer's notebook; opinion; imagination; reason; experience; mind; work; academia; criticism

De stylo, et optimo scribendi genere. – For a man to write well, there are required three necessaries – to read the best authors, observe the best speakers, and much exercise of his own style; in style to consider what ought to be written, and after what manner. He must first think and excogitate his matter, then choose his words, and examine the weight of either. Then take care, in placing and ranking both matter and words, that the composition be comely; and to do this with diligence and often. No matter how slow the style be at first, so it be laboured and accurate; seek the best, and be not glad of the froward conceits, or first words, that offer themselves to us; but judge of what we invent, and order what we approve. Repeat often what we have formerly written; which beside that it helps the consequence, and makes the juncture better, it quickens the heat of imagination, that often cools in the time of setting down, and gives it new strength…For all that we invent doth please us in conception of birth, else we would never set it down. But the safest is to return to our judgment, and handle over again those things, the easiness of which might make them justly suspected. So did the best writers in their beginnings; they imposed upon themselves care and industry; they did nothing rashly: they obtained first to write well, and then custom made it easy and a habit. By little and little their matter showed itself to them more plentifully; their words answered, their composition followed…So that the sum of all is, ready writing makes not good writing, but good writing brings on ready writing yet, when we think we have got the faculty, it is even then good to resist it…Again, whether a man's genius is best able to reach thither, it should more and more contend, lift and dilate itself, as men of low stature raise themselves on their toes…Besides, as it is fit for grown and able writers to stand of themselves, and work with their own strength, to trust and endeavour by their own faculties, so it is fit for the beginner and learner to study others and the best. For the mind and memory are more sharply exercised in comprehending another man's things than our own; and such as accustom themselves and are familiar with the best authors shall ever and anon find somewhat of them in themselves, and in the expression of their minds, even when they feel it not, be able to utter something like theirs, which hath an authority above their own…

style; writing; reading; study; intertextuality; genius; pedagogy; structure; imitation; learning; practice

What is a Poet?

Poeta. – A poet is that which by the Greeks is called a maker, or a feigner: his art, an art of imitation of feigning; expressing the life of man in fit measures, numbers, and harmony, according to Aristotle…Hence he is called a poet, not he which writeth in measure only, but that feigneth and formeth a fable, and writes things like the truth. For the fable and fiction is, as it were, the form and soul of any poetical work or poem.

What mean you by a Poem?

Poema. – A poem is not alone any work or composition of the poet's in many or few verses; but even one verse alone sometimes makes a perfect poem…

Virorum schola respub. – The poet is the nearest borderer upon the orator, and expresseth all his virtues, though he be tied more to numbers, is his equal in ornament, and above him in his strengths…

To judge of poets is only the faculty of poets; and not of all poets, but the best…But some will say critics are a kind of tinkers, that make more faults than they mend ordinarily. See their diseases and those of grammarians. It is true, many bodies are the worse for the meddling with; and the multitude of physicians hath destroyed many sound patients with their wrong practice. But the office of a true critic or censor is, not to throw by a letter anywhere, or damn an innocent syllable, but lay the words together, and amend them; judge sincerely of the author and his matter, which is the sign of solid and perfect learning in a man.

Of the magnitude and compass of any fable, epic or dramatic.

What the measure of a fable is. – The fable or plot of a poem defined... To the resolving of this question we must first agree in the definition of the fable. The fable is called the imitation of one entire and perfect action, whose parts are so joined and knit together, as nothing in the structure can be changed, or taken away, without impairing or troubling the whole, of which there is a proportionable magnitude in the members...

critic; poet; judgement; story; plot; structure; truth; thought; narrative

JOHN MILTON (1608–1674)

OF EDUCATION *(1644)*

The end…of Learning is to repair the ruines of our first Parents by regaining to know God aright, and out of that knowledge to love him, to imitate him, to be like him, as we may the nearest by possessing our souls of true virtue, which being united to the heavenly grace of faith makes up the highest perfection. But because our understanding cannot in this body found it self but on sensible things, nor arrive so clearly to the knowledge of God and things invisible, as by orderly conning over the visible and inferior creature, the same method is necessarily to be follow'd in all discreet teaching.

First, to find out a spatious house and ground about it fit for an *Academy*, and big enough to lodge a hundred and fifty persons, whereof twenty or thereabout may be attendants, all under the government of one, who shall be thought of desert sufficient and ability to do all, or wisely to direct, and oversee it done. This place should be at once both Scholl and University, not needing a remove to any other house of Schollership, except it be some peculiar Colledge of Law, or Physick, where they mean to be practitioners; but as for those general studies which take up all our time from *Lilly* to the commencing, as they term it, Master of Art, it should be absolute. After this pattern, as many Edifices may be converted to this use, as shall be needful in every City throughout this Land, which would tend much to the encrease of Learning and Civility everywhere...

For their studies, First they should begin with the chief and necessary rules of some good Grammar, either that now us'd, or any better: and while this is doing, their speech is to be fashion'd to a distinct and clear pronunciation, as near as may be to the Italian, especially in the Vowels. For we Englishmen being far northerly, do not open our mouths in the cold air, wide enough to grace a Southern Tongue; but are observed by all other Nations to speak exceeding close and inward... Next to make them expert in the usefullest points of Grammar, and withall to season them, and win them early to the love of vertue and true labour, ere any flattering seducement or vain principle seise them wandering, some easie and delightful Book of Education would be read to them...But here the main skill and groundwork will be, to temper them such Lectures and Explanations upon every opportunity as may lead and draw them in willing obedience, inflamed with the study of Learning, and the admiration of Vertue; stirred up with high hopes of living to be brave men, and worthy Patriots, dear to God, and famous to all ages. That they may despise and scorn all their childish and ill-taught qualities, to delight in manly, and liberall Exercises: which he who hath the Art, and proper Eloquence to catch them with, what with mild and effectual perswasions, and what with the intimation of some fear, if need be, but chiefly by his own example, might in a short space gain them to an incredible diligence and courage: infusing into their young brests such an ingenuous and noble ardor, as would not fail to make many of them renowned and matchless men. At the same time, some other hour of the day, might be taught them the rules of Arithmetick, and soon after the Elements of Geometry…After evening repast, till bedtime their thoughts will best be taken up in the easie grounds of Religion and the story of Scripture…

…The next remove must be to the study of *Politicks*; to know the beginning, end, and reasons of Political Societies; that they may (be)…stedfast pillars of the State…Sundayes also and every evening may be now understandingly spent in the highest matters of *Theology*, and Church History ancient and modern; and ere this time the Hebrew Tongue at a set hour might have been gain'd, that the Scriptures may be now read in their own original…And now lastly will be the time to read with them those organic arts which inable men to discourse and write perspicuously, elegantly, and according to the fitted stile of lofty, mean, or lowly. Logic therefore so much as is useful…until it be time to open her contracted palm into a gracefull and ornate Rhetorick taught out of the rule of Plato, Aristotle…To which Poetry would be made subsequent, or indeed rather precedent. as being less suttle and fine, but more simple, sensuous and passionate…(to) shew them, what religious, what glorious and magnificent use might be made of Poetry both in divine and humane things. From hence and not till now will be the right season of forming them to be able Writers and Composers in every excellent matter, when they shall be thus fraught with an universal insight into things…These are the Studies wherein our noble and our gentle Youth ought to bestow their time in a disciplinary way from twelve to one and twenty…

the divine; education; language; academy; grammar; enunciation; morality; reading; gender; poetry; rhetoric; theology; politics; religion

AREOPAGITICA: *a speech of Mr John Milton for the liberty of unlicensed printing to the Parliament of England (1644)*

...If ye be thus resolved, as it were injury to think ye were not, I know not what should withhold me from presenting ye with a first instance wherein to show both that love of truth which ye eminently profess, and that uprightness of your judgment which is not wont to be partial to yourselves; by judging over again that order which ye have ordained to regulate printing: – that no book, pamphlet, or paper shall be henceforth printed, unless the same be first approved and licensed by such, or at least one of such, as shall be thereto appointed. For that part which preserves justly every man's copy to himself, or provides for the poor, I touch not, only wish they be not made pretences to abuse and persecute honest and painful men, who offend not in either of these particulars. But that other clause of licensing books, which we thought had died with his brother quadragesimal and matrimonial when the prelates expired, I shall now attend with such a homily, as shall lay before ye, first the inventors of it to be those whom ye will loath to own; next what is to be thought in general of reading, whatever sort the books be; and that this Order avails nothing to the suppressing of scandalous, seditious and libellous books, which were mainly intended to be suppressed. Last, that it will be primely to the discouragement of all learning, and the stop of truth, not only by disexercising and blunting our abilities in what we know already, but by hindering and cropping the discovery that might be yet further made both in religious and civil wisdom...

I deny not, but that it is of greatest concernment in the Church and Commonwealth, to have a vigilant eye how books demean themselves as well as men…For books are not absolutely dead things, but do contain a potency of life in them to be as active as that soul was whose progeny they are…I know they are as lively, and as vigorously productive, as those fabulous dragon's teeth; and being sown up and down, may chance to spring up armed men. And yet, on the other hand, unless wariness be used, as good almost kill a man as kill a good book. Who kills a man kills a reasonable creature, God's image; but he who destroys a good book, kills reason itself; kills the image of God, as it were, in the eye. Many a man lives a burden to the earth; but a good book is the previous life-blood of a master spirit, embalmed and treasured up on purpose to a life beyond life…

…For books are as meats and viands are; some of good, some of evil substance; and yet God, in that unapocryphal vision, said without exception, RISE, PETER, KILL AND EAT, leaving the choice to each man's discretion. Wholesome meats to a vitiated stomach differ little or nothing from unwholesome; and best books to a naughty mind are not unappliable to occasions of evil. Bad meats will scarce breed good nourishment in the healthiest concoction; but herein the difference is of bad books, that they to a discreet and judicious reader serve in many respects to confute, to forewarn and to illustrate…I conceive, therefore, that when God did enlarge the universal diet of man's body, saving ever the rules of temperance, he then also, as before, left arbitrary the dieting and repasting of our minds; as wherein every mature man might have to exercise his own leading capacity.

…Besides another inconvenience, if learned men be the first receivers out of books and dispreaders, both of vice and error, how shall the licensers themselves be confided in, unless we can confer on them, or they assume to themselves above all others in the land, the grace of infallibility and uncorruptedness? And again, if it be true that a wise man, like a good refiner, can gather gold out of the drossiest volume, and that a fool will be a fool with the best book, yea or without book; there is no reason that we should deprive a wise man of any advantage to his wisdom, while we seek to restrain from a fool, that which being restrained will be no hindrance to his folly...

Another reason whereby to make it plain that this Order will miss the end it seeks, consider by the quality which ought to be in every licenser. It cannot be denied but that he who is made judge to sit upon the birth or death of books, whether they may be wafted into this world or not, had need to be a man above the common measure, both studious, learned, and judicious; there may be else no mean mistakes in the censure of what is passable or not; which is also no mean injury. If he be of such worth as behoves him, there cannot be a more tedious and unpleasing journey-work, a greater loss of time levied upon his head, than to be made the perpetual reader of unchosen books and pamphlets, ofttimes huge volumes. There is no book that is acceptable unless at certain seasons; but to be enjoined the reading of that at all times, and in a hand scarce legible, whereof three pages would not down at any time in the fairest print, is an imposition which I cannot believe how he that values time and his own studies, or is but of a sensible nostril, should be able to endure...

...When a man writes to the world, he summons up all his reason and deliberation to assist him; he searches, meditates, is industrious, and likely consults and confers with his judicious friends; after all which done he takes himself to be informed in what he writes, as well as any that writ before him. If, in this the most consummate act of his fidelity and ripeness, no years, no industry, no former proof of his abilities can bring him to that state of maturity, as not to be still mistrusted and suspected, unless he carry all his considerate diligence, all his midnight watchings and expense of Palladian oil, to the hasty view of an unleisured licenser, perhaps much his younger, perhaps his inferior in judgement, perhaps one who never knew the labour of bookwriting, and if he be not repulsed or slighted, must appear in print with his guardian, and his censor's hand on the back of his title to be his bail and surety that he is no idiot or seducer, it cannot be but a dishonour and derogation to the author, to the book, to the privilege and dignity of learning…

And how can a man teach with authority, which is the life of teaching; how can he be a doctor in his book as he ought to be, or else had better be silent, whenas all he teaches, all he delivers, is but under the tuition, under the correction of his patriarchal licenser to blot or alter what precisely accords not with the hidebound humour which he calls his judgement? When every acute reader, upon the first sight of a pedantic licence, will be ready with these like words to ding the book a quoit's distance from him: I hate a pupil teacher, I endure not an instructor that comes to me under the wardship of an overseeing fist…

Nor is it to the common people less than a reproach; for if we be so jealous over them, as that we dare not trust them with an English pamphlet, what do we but censure them for a giddy, vicious, and ungrounded people; in such a sick and weak state of faith and discretion, as to be able to take nothing down but through the pipe of a licenser?…

And lest some should persuade ye, Lords and Commons, that these arguments of learned men's discouragement at this your Order are mere flourishes, and not real, I could recount what I have seen and heard in other countries, where this kind of inquisition tyrannises; when I have sat among their learned men, for that honour I had, and been counted happy to be born in such a place of philosophic freedom, as they supposed England was, while themselves did nothing but bemoan the servile condition into which learning amongst them was brought; that this was it which had damped the glory of Italian wits; that nothing had been here written now these many years but flattery and fustian. There it was that I found and visited the famous Galileo, grown old, a prisoner to the Inquisition, for thinking in astronomy otherwise than the Franciscan and Dominican licensers thought...

Well knows he who uses to consider, that our faith and knowledge thrives by exercise, as well as our limbs and complexion. Truth is compared in Scripture to a streaming fountain; if her waters flow not in a perpetual progression, they sicken into a muddy pool of conformity and tradition.

printing; censorship; copyright; author; truth; intellectual property rights; reason; morality; books; reading; teaching

JOHN DRYDEN (1631–1700)

OF DRAMATICK POESIE AN ESSAY *(1668)*

(9) …how was it possible to be decided who writ the best Plays, before we know what a Play should be?

[16] …I must remember you that all the Rules by which we practise the Drama at this day, either such as relate to the justness and symmetry of the Plot; or the Episodical Ornaments, such as Descriptions, Narrations, and other Beauties, which are not essential to the Play; were delivered to us from the Observations that Aristotle made, of those Poets, which either liv'd before him, or were his Contemporaries: we have added nothing of our own, except we have the confidence to say our wit is better; which none boast of in our Age, but such as understand not theirs.

[17] …the Famous Rules which the French call, *Des Trois Vnitez*, or, The Three Unities, which ought to be observ'd in every Regular Play; namely, of Time, Place, and Action.

[18] The unity of Time they comprehend in 24 hours, the

compass of a Natural Day; or as near it as can be contriv'd: and the reason of it is obvious to every one, that the time of the feigned action, or fable of the Play, should be proportion'd as near as can be to the duration of that time in which it is represented; since therefore all Playes are acted on the Theater in a space of time much within the compass of 24 hours, that Play is to be thought the nearest imitation of Nature, whose Plot or Action is confin'd within that time; and, by the same Rule which concludes this general proportion of time, it follows, that all the parts of it are to be equally subdivided; as namely, that one act take not up the suppos'd time of half a day; which is out of proportion to the rest: since the other four are then to be straightened within the compas of the remaining half; for it is unnatural that one Act, which being spoke or written, is not longer than the rest, should be suppos'd longer by the Audience; 'tis therefore the Poets duty, to take care that no Act should be imagin'd to exceed the time in which it is represented on the Stage, and that the intervalls and inequalities of time be suppos'd to fall out between the Acts.

[19] This Rule of Time how well it has been observ'd by the Antients, most of their Playes will witness; you see them in their Tragedies (wherein to follow this Rule, is certainly most difficult) from the very beginning of their Playes, falling close into that part of the Story which they intend for the action or principal object of it; leaving the former part to be delivered by Narration: so that they set the Audience, as it were, at the Post where the Race is to be concluded: and, saving them the tedious expectation of seeing the Poet set out and ride the beginning of the Course, you behold him not, till he is in sight of the Goal, and just upon you.

[20] For the Second Unity, which is that of place, the Antients meant by it, That the Scene ought to be continu'd through the Play, in the same place where it was laid in the beginning: for the Stage, on which it is represented, being but one and the same place, it is unnatural to conceive it many; and those far distant from one another. I will not deny but by the variation of painted Scenes, the Fancy (which in these cases will contribute to its own deceit) may sometimes imagine it several places, with some appearance of probability; yet it still carries the greater likelihood of truth, if those places be suppos'd so near each other, as in the same Town or City; which may all be comprehended under the larger Denomination of one place: for a greater distance will bear no proportion to the shortness of time, which is allotted in the acting, to pass from one of them to another; for the Observation of this, next to the Antients, the French are to be most commended. They tie themselves so strictly to the unity of place, that you never see in any of their Plays a Scene chang'd in the middle of the Act: if the Act begins in a Garden, a Street, or Chamber, 'tis ended in the same place; and that you may know it to be the same, the Stage is so supplied with persons that it is never empty all the time: he that enters the second has business with him who was on before; and before the second quits the Stage, a third appears who has business with him.

[22] As for the third Unity which is that of Action, the Ancients meant no other by it then what the Logicians do by their *Finis*, the end or scope of an action: that which is the first in Intention, and last in Execution: now the Poet is to aim at one great and compleat action, to the carrying on of which all things in his Play, even the very obstacles, are to be subservient; and the reason of this is as evident as any of the former.

[36] But in how straight a compass soever they have bounded their Plots and Characters, we will pass it by, if they have regularly pursued them, and perfectly observ'd those three Unities of Time, Place, and Action: the knowledge of which you say is deriv'd to us from them. But in the first place give me leave to tell you, that the Unity of Place, how ever it might be practised by them, was never any of their Rules: We neither find it in Aristotle, Horace, or any who have written of it, till in our age the French Poets first made it a Precept of the Stage.

value judgement; genre; plot; Unities; tragedy; structure; action; character

PART THREE

Eighteenth Century

STATUTE OF ANNE (1709–1710)

An Act for the Encouragement of Learning, by vesting the Copies of Printed Books in the Authors or purchasers of such Copies, during the Times therein mentioned.

Whereas printers, booksellers, and other persons have of late frequently taken the liberty of printing, reprinting, and publishing, or causing to be printed, reprinted, and published, books and other writings, without the consent of the authors or proprietors of such books and writings, to their very great detriment, and too often to the ruin of them and their families: for preventing therefore such practices for the future, and for the encouragement of learned men to compose and write useful books; may it please your Majesty, that it may be enacted, and be it enacted by the Queen's most excellent majesty, by and with the advice and consent of the lords spiritual and temporal, and commons, in this present parliament assembled, and by the authority of the same;

That from and after the tenth day of April, one thousand seven hundred and ten, the author of any book or books already printed, who hath not transferred to any other the copy or copies of such book or books, share or shares thereof, or the bookseller or booksellers, printer or printers, or other person or persons, who hath or have purchased or acquired the copy or copies of any book or books, in order to print or reprint the same, shall have the sole right and liberty of printing such book and books for the term of one and twenty years, to commence from the said tenth day of April, and no longer; and That the author of any book or books already composed, and not printed and published, or that shall hereafter be composed, and his assignee or assigns, shall have the sole liberty of printing and reprinting such book and books for the term of fourteen years, to commence from the day of the first publishing the same, and no longer; and That if any other bookseller, printer or other person whatsoever, from and after the tenth day of April, one thousand seven hundred and ten, within the times granted and limited by this act, as aforesaid, shall print, reprint, or import, or cause to be printed, reprinted, or imported, any such book or books, without the consent of the proprietor or proprietors thereof first had and obtained in writing, signed in the presence of two or more credible witnesses; or knowing the same to be so printed or reprinted, without the consent of the proprietors, shall sell, publish, or expose to sale, or cause to be sold, published or exposed to sale, any such book or books, without such consent first had and obtained, as aforesaid: then such offender or offenders shall forfeit such book or books, and all and every sheet or sheets, being part of such book or books, to the proprietor or proprietors of the copy thereof, who shall forthwith damask, and make waste paper of them…

V. Provided always, and it is hereby enacted, That nine copies of each book or books, upon the best paper, that from and after the said tenth day of April, one thousand seven hundred and ten, shall be printed and published, as aforesaid, or reprinted and published with additions, shall, by the printer and printers thereof, be delivered to the warehouse keeper of the said company of stationers for the time being, at the hall of the said company, before such publication made, for the use of the royal library, the libraries of the universities of Oxford and Cambridge, the libraries of the four universities in Scotland, the library of Sion College in London, and the library commonly called the library belonging to the faculty of advocates at Edinburgh respectively...

X1. Provided always, That after the expiration of the said term of fourteen years, the sole right of printing or disposing of copies shall return to the authors thereof, if they are then living, for another term of fourteen years.

copyright; learning; printing; author; censorship; publishing

ALEXANDER POPE
(1688–1744)

———————————

AN ESSAY ON CRITICISM *(1711)*

PART ONE

'Tis with our judgments as our watches, none
Go just alike, yet each believes his own
In poets as true genius is but rare
True tast as seldom is the critic share
Both must alike from Heaven derive their light,
These born to judge as well as those to write
Let such teach others who themselves excel,
And censure freely, who have written well
Authors are partial to their wit, 'tis true
But are not critics to their judgement too?
…
Some have at first for wits then poets passed
Turned critics next and proved plain fools at last
Some neither can for wits nor critics pass
As heavy mules are neither horse nor ass.
Those half-learned witlings, numerous in our isle,
As half-formed insects on the banks of Nile

Unfinished things one knows not what to call
Their generation is so equivocal
To tell them would a hundred tongues require,
Or one vain wit that might a hundred tire.

But you who seek to give and merit fame.
And justly bear a critic's noble name,
Be sure yourself and your own reach to go,
Launch not beyond your depth, but be discreet
And mark that point where sense and dullness meet.
…
First follow nature and your judgment frame
By her just standard, which is still the same.
Unerring nature still divinely bright,
One clear, unchanged and universal light,
Life force and beauty, must to all impart
At once the source and end and test of art
Art from that fund each just supply provides,
Works without show and without pomp presides
In some fair body thus the informing soul
With spirits feeds, with vigor fills the whole,
Each motion guides and every nerve sustains,
Itself unseen, but in the effects remains.
Some, to whom Heaven in wit has been profuse,
Want as much more, to turn it to its use;
For wit and judgment often are at strife,
Though meant each other's aid, like man and wife.
'Tis more to guide, than spur the muse's steed,
Restrain his fury, than provoke his speed,
The winged courser, like a generous horse,
Shows most true mettle when you check his course.

...

You then, whose judgment the right course would steer,
Know well each ancient's proper character.
His fable subject scope in every page,
Religion, country, genius of his age
Without all these at once before your eyes,
Cavil you may, but never criticise.
Be Homers works your study and delight,
Read them by day and meditate by night,
Thence form your judgement thence your maxims bring
And trace the muses upwards to their spring.

...

Some beauties yet no precepts can declare,
For there's a happiness as well as care.
Music resembles poetry – in each
Are nameless graces which no methods teach,
And which a master hand alone can reach
If, where the rules not far enough extent
(Since rules were made but to promote their end),
The intent proposed that license is a rule.

judgement; poet; genius; critic; muse; beauty; context; influence; wit; the natural; learning; inspiration; criticism

PART TWO

A little learning is a dangerous thing
Drink deep, or taste not the Pierian spring
There shallow draughts intoxicate the brain,
And drinking largely sobers us again.
Fired at first sight with what the muse imparts,

In fearless youth we tempt the heights of arts
While from the bounded level of our mind
Short views we take nor see the lengths behind
But more advanced behold with strange surprise,
New distant scenes of endless science rise!

judgement; pride; reason; truth; knowledge; learning; muse

...

A perfect judge will read each work of wit
With the same spirit that its author writ,
Survey the whole nor seek slight faults to find
Where nature moves and rapture warms the mind,
Nor lose for that malignant dull delight
The generous pleasure to be charmed with wit
But in such lays as neither ebb nor flow,
Correctly cold and regularly low
That, shunning faults, one quiet tenor keep;
We cannot blame indeed – but we may sleep.
In wit, as nature, what affects our hearts
Is not the exactness of peculiar part,
'Tis not a lip, or eye, we beauty call,
But the joint force and full result of all.

...

Whoever thinks a faultless piece to see,
Thinks what ne'er was, nor is, nor e'er shall be.
In every work regard the writer's end,
Since none can compass more than they intend;
And if the means be just, the conduct true,
Applause, in spite of trivial faults, is due.
As men of breeding, sometimes men of wit,

To avoid great errors, must the less commit:
Neglect the rules each verbal critic lays,
For not to know some trifles is a praise.
Most critics, fond of some subservient art,
Still make the whole depend upon a part:
They talk of principles, but notions prize,
And all to one loved folly sacrifice.

intention; criticism; structure; beauty; perfection

JOSEPH ADDISON (1672–1719)

The Spectator, No 412, Monday, June 23, 1712.

I shall first consider those Pleasures of the Imagination, which arise from the actual View and Survey of outward Objects: And these, I think, all proceed from the Sight of what is Great, Uncommon, or Beautiful. There may, indeed, be something so terrible or offensive, that the Horror or Loathsomeness of an Object may over-bear the Pleasure which results from its Greatness, Novelty, or Beauty; but still there will be such a Mixture of Delight in the very Disgust it gives us, as any of these three Qualifications are most conspicuous and prevailing.

By Greatness, I do not only mean the Bulk of any single Object, but the Largeness of a whole View, considered as one entire Piece. Such are the Prospects of an open Champain Country, a vast uncultivated Desart, of huge Heaps of Mountains, high Rocks and Precipices, or a wide Expanse of Waters, where we are not struck with the Novelty or Beauty of the Sight, but with that rude kind of Magnificence which appears in many of these stupendous Works of Nature. Our Imagination loves to be filled with an Object, or to grasp at any thing that is too big for its Capacity. We are flung into a pleasing

Astonishment at such unbounded Views, and feel a delightful Stillness and Amazement in the Soul at the Apprehension[s] of them. The Mind of Man naturally hates every thing that looks like a Restraint upon it, and is apt to fancy it self under a sort of Confinement, when the Sight is pent up in a narrow Compass, and shortend on every side by the Neighbourhood of Walls or Mountains. On the contrary, a spacious Horizon is an Image of Liberty, where the Eye has Room to range abroad, to expatiate at large on the Immensity of its Views, and to lose it self amidst the Variety of Objects that offer themselves to its Observation. Such wide and undetermined Prospects are as pleasing to the Fancy, as the Speculations of Eternity or Infinitude are to the Understanding. But if there be a Beauty or Uncommonness joined with this Grandeur, as in a troubled Ocean, a Heaven adorned with Stars and Meteors, or a spacious Landskip cut out into Rivers, Woods, Rocks, and Meadows, the Pleasure still grows upon us, as it rises from more than a single Principle.

Every thing that is new or uncommon raises a Pleasure in the Imagination, because it fills the Soul with an agreeable Surprize, gratifies its Curiosity, and gives it an Idea of which it was not before possest. We are indeed so often conversant with one Set of Objects, and tired out with so many repeated Shows of the same Things, that whatever is new or uncommon contributes a little to vary human Life, and to divert our Minds, for a while, with the Strangeness of its Appearance:

It serves us for a kind of Refreshment, and takes off from that Satiety we are apt to complain of in our usual and ordinary Entertainments. It is this that bestows Charms on a Monster, and makes even the Imperfections of Nature [please [1]] us. It is this that recommends Variety, where the Mind is every Instant called off to something new, and the Attention not suffered to dwell too long, and waste it self on any particular Object. It is this, likewise, that improves what is great or beautiful, and make it afford the Mind a double Entertainment. Groves, Fields, and Meadows, are at any Season of the Year pleasant to look upon, but never so much as in the Opening of the Spring, when they are all new and fresh, with their first Gloss upon them, and not yet too much accustomed and familiar to the Eye. For this Reason there is nothing that more enlivens a Prospect than Rivers, Jetteaus, or Falls of Water, where the Scene is perpetually shifting, and entertaining the Sight every Moment with something that is new. We are quickly tired with looking upon Hills and Vallies, where every thing continues fixed and settled in the same Place and Posture, but find our Thoughts a little agitated and relieved at the Sight of such Objects as are ever in Motion, and sliding away from beneath the Eye of the Beholder.

imagination; beauty; pleasure; grandeur; fancy; revulsion; structure; novelty; curiosity; variety; aesthetics

ANNE FINCH (KINGSMILL), COUNTESS OF WINCHILSEA (1661–1720)

Miscellany poems (1713)

THE INTRODUCTION

Did I, my lines intend for publick view,
How many censures, wou'd their faults persue,
Some wou'd, because such words they do affect,
Cry they're insipid, empty, uncorrect.
And many, have attain'd, dull and untaught
The name of Witt, only by finding fault.
True judges, might condemn their want of witt,
And all might say, they're by a Woman writt.
Alas! a woman that attempts the pen,
Such an intruder on the rights of men,
Such a presumptuous Creature, is esteem'd,
The fault, can by no vertue be redeem'd.
They tell us, we mistake our sex and way;
Good breeding, fassion, dancing, dressing, play
Are the accomplishments we shou'd desire;

To write, or read, or think, or to enquire
Wou'd cloud our beauty, and exaust our time;
And interrupt the Conquests of our prime;
Whilst the dull mannage, of a servile house
Is held by some, our outmost art, and use.
Sure 'twas not ever thus, nor are we told
Fables, of Women that excell'd of old;
To whom, by the diffusive hand of Heaven
Some share of witt, and poetry was given.
On that glad day, on which the Ark return'd,
The holy pledge, for which the Land had mourn'd,
The joyfull Tribes, attend itt on the way,
The Levites do the sacred Charge convey,
Whilst various Instruments, before itt play;
Here, holy Virgins in the Concert joyn,
The louder notes, to soften, and refine,
And with alternate verse, compleat the Hymn Devine.
Loe! the yong Poet, after Gods own heart,
By Him inspired, and taught the Muses Art,
Return'd from Conquest, a bright Chorus meets,
That sing his slayn ten thousand in the streets.
In such loud numbers they his acts declare,
Proclaim the wonders, of his early war,
That Saul upon the vast applause does frown,
And feels, itts mighty thunder shake the Crown.
What, can the threat'n'd Judgment now prolong?
Half of the Kingdom is already gone;
The fairest half, whose influence guides the rest,
Have David's Empire, o're their hearts confess't.
A Woman here, leads fainting Israel on,
She fights, she wins, she tryumphs with a song,

Devout, Majestick, for the subject fitt,
And far above her arms, exalts her witt,
Then, to the peacefull, shady Palm withdraws,
And rules the rescu'd Nation with her Laws.
How are we fal'n, fal'n by mistaken rules?
And Education's, more than Nature's fools,
Debarr'd from all improve-ments of the mind,
And to be dull, expected and dessigned;
And if some one, would Soar above the rest,
With warmer fancy, and ambition press't,
So strong, th' opposing faction still appears,
The hopes to thrive, can ne're outweigh the fears,
Be caution'd then my Muse, and still retir'd;
Nor be dispis'd, aiming to be admir'd;
Conscious of wants, still with contracted wing,
To some few freinds, and to thy sorrows sing;
For groves of Lawrell, thou wert never meant;
Be dark enough thy shades, and be thou there content.

publication; judgement; women; gender; prejudice; inspiration;
the Muse; education

SAMUEL JOHNSON
(1709–1784)

PREFACE TO A DICTIONARY OF THE ENGLISH LANGUAGE *(1755)*

It is the fate of those who toil at the lower employments of life, to be rather driven by the fear of evil, than attracted by the prospect of good; to be exposed to censure, without hope of praise; to be disgraced by miscarriage, or punished for neglect, where success would have been without applause, and diligence without reward.

Among these unhappy mortals is the writer of dictionaries; whom mankind have considered, not as the pupil, but the slave of science, the pioneer of literature, doomed only to remove rubbish and clear obstructions from the paths through which Learning and Genius press forward to conquest and glory, without bestowing a smile on the humble drudge that facilitates their progress. Every other authour may aspire to praise; the lexicographer can only hope to escape reproach, and even this negative recompense has been yet granted to very few.

I have, notwithstanding this discouragement, attempted a dictionary of the English language, which, while it was employed in the cultivation of every species of literature, has itself been hitherto neglected; suffered to spread, under the direction of chance into wild exuberance; resigned to the tyranny of time and fashion; and exposed to the corruptions of ignorance, and caprices of innovation.

When I took the first survey of my undertaking, I found our speech copious without order, and energetick without rules: wherever I turned my view, there was perplexity to be disentangled, and confusion to be regulated; choice was to be made out of boundless variety, without any established principle of selection; adulterations were to be detected, without a settled test of purity; and modes of expression to be rejected or received, without the suffrages of any writers of classical reputation or acknowledged authority...

As language was at its beginning merely oral, all words of necessary or common use were spoken before they were written; and while they were unfixed by any visible signs, must have been spoken with great diversity, as we now observe those who cannot read catch sounds imperfectly, and utter them negligently. When this wild and barbarous jargon was first reduced to an alphabet, every penman endeavoured to express, as he could, the sounds which he was accustomed to pronounce or receive, and vitiated in writing such words as were already vitiated in speech. The powers of the letters, when they were applied to the new language, must have been vague and unsettled, and therefore different hands would exhibit the same sound by different combinations.

From this uncertain pronunciation arise in a great part the various dialects of the same country, which will always be observed to grow fewer, and less different, as books are multiplied; and from this arbitrary representation of sounds by letters, proceeds that diversity of spelling observable in the

Saxon remains, and I suppose in the first books of every nation, which perplexes or destroys analogy, and produces anomalous formations, that, being once incorporated, can never be afterward dismissed or reformed...

It has been asserted, that for the law to be KNOWN, is of more importance than to be RIGHT...There is in constancy and stability a general and lasting advantage, which will always overbalance the slow improvements of gradual correction. Much less ought our written language to comply with the corruptions of oral utterance, or copy that which every variation of time or place makes different from itself, and imitate those changes, which will again be changed, while imitation is employed in observing them.

This recommendation of steadiness and uniformity does not proceed from an opinion, that particular combinations of letters have much influence on human happiness; or that truth may not be successfully taught by modes of spelling fanciful and erroneous: am not yet so lost in lexicography, as to forget that WORDS ARE THE DAUGHTERS OF EARTH, AND THAT THINGS ARE THE SONS OF HEAVEN. Language is only the instrument of science, and words are but the signs of ideas: I wish, however, that the instrument might be less apt to decay, and that signs might be permanent, like the things which they denote...

But to COLLECT the WORDS of our language was a task of greater difficulty: the deficiency of dictionaries was immediately apparent; and when they were exhausted, what was yet wanting must be sought by fortuitous and unguided excursions into books, and gleaned as industry should find, or chance should offer it, in the boundless chaos of a living speech. My search, however, has been either skilful or lucky; for I have much augmented the vocabulary...

That part of my work on which I expect malignity most frequently to fasten, is the explanation; in which I cannot hope to satisfy those, who are perhaps not inclined to be pleased, since I have not always been able to satisfy myself. To interpret a language by itself is very difficult; many words cannot be explained by synonimes, because the idea signified by them has not more than one appellation; nor by paraphrase, because simple ideas cannot be described. When the nature of things is unknown, or the notion unsettled and indefinite, and various in various minds, the words by which such notions are conveyed, or such things denoted, will be ambiguous and perplexed. And such is the fate of hapless lexicography, that not only darkness, but light, impedes and distresses it; things may be not only too little, but too much known, to be happily illustrated. To explain, requires the use of terms less abstruse than that which is to be explained, and such terms cannot always be found; for as nothing can be proved but by supposing something intuitively known, and evident without proof, so nothing can be defined but by the use of words too plain to admit a definition...

The chief glory of every people arises from its authours: whether I shall add any thing by my own writings to the reputation of English literature, must be left to time: much of my life has been lost under the pressures of disease; much has been trifled away; and much has always been spent in provision for the day that was passing over me; but I shall not think my employment useless or ignoble, if by my assistance foreign nations, and distant ages, gain access to the propagators of knowledge, and understand the teachers of truth; if my labours afford light to the repositories of science, and add celebrity to Bacon, to Hooker, to Milton, and to Boyle.

When I am animated by this wish, I look with pleasure

on my book, however defective, and deliver it to the world with the spirit of a man that has endeavoured well. That it will immediately become popular I have not promised to myself: a few wild blunders, and risible absurdities, from which no work of such multiplicity was ever free, may for a time furnish forth folly with laughter, and harden ignorance in contempt; but useful diligence will at last prevail, and there never can be wanting some who distinguish desert; who will consider that no dictionary of a living tongue ever can be perfect, since while it is hastening to publication, some words are budding, and some falling away; that a whole life cannot be spent upon syntax and etymology, and that even a whole life would not be sufficient; that he, whose design includes whatever language can express, must often speak of what he does not understand; that a writer will sometimes be hurried by eagerness to the end, and sometimes faint with weariness...that what is obvious is not always known, and what is known is not always present; that sudden fits of advertency will surprise vigilance, slight avocations will seduce attention, and casual eclipses of the mind will darken learning; and that the writer shall often in vain trace his memory at the moment of need, for that which yesterday he knew with intuitive readiness, and which will come uncalled into his thoughts tomorrow.

dictionary; language; judgement; innovation; literature; meaning; grammar; oracy; literacy; dialect; standard English; science; genius; arbitrariness of sounds; printing; rules; consistency; gender; ideas; signs; synonyms; paraphrase; philosophy; research; words; things; lexicography; tradition; rules; conventions

EDMUND BURKE (1729–1797)

A philosophical enquiry into the origin of our ideas of the sublime and the beautiful (1756-7)

Part 1, Section 11, Pain and Pleasure

…Pain and pleasure are simple ideas, incapable of definition. People are not liable to be mistaken in their feelings, but they are very frequently wrong in the names they give them, and in their reasonings about them. Many are of opinion, that pain arises necessarily from the removal of some pleasure; as they think pleasure does from the ceasing or diminution of some pain. For my part, I am rather inclined to imagine, that pain and pleasure, in their most simple and natural manner of affecting, are each of a positive nature, and by no means necessarily dependent on each other for their existence. The human mind is often, and I think it is for the most part, in a state neither of pain nor pleasure, which I call a state of indifference. When I am carried from this state into a state of actual pleasure, it does not appear necessary that I should pass through the medium of any sort of pain. If in such a state of indifference, or ease, or tranquillity, or call it what you please, you were to be suddenly entertained with a concert of music; or suppose some object of a fine shape, and bright, lively colours, to be presented before you; or imagine your smell is gratified with the fragrance of a rose; or if, without any previous thirst, you were to drink of some pleasant kind of wine, or to taste of some sweetmeat without being hungry; in all the several senses, of hearing, smelling, and tasting, you undoubtedly find a pleasure; yet, if I inquire into the state of your mind previous to these gratifications, you will hardly tell me that they found you in any kind of pain; or, having satisfied these several senses with their several pleasures, will you say that any pain has succeeded, though the pleasure is absolutely over? Suppose, on the other hand, a man in the same state of indifference to receive a violent blow, or to drink of some bitter potion, or to have his ears wounded with some harsh and grating sound; here is no removal of pleasure; and yet here is felt, his every sense which is affected, a pain very distinguishable. It may be said, perhaps, that the pain in these cases had its rise from the removal of the pleasure which the man enjoyed before, though that pleasure was of so low a degree as to be perceived only by the removal. But this seems to me a subtilty that is not discoverable in nature. For if, previous to the pain, I do not feel any actual pleasure, I have no reason to judge that any such thing exists; since pleasure is only pleasure as it is felt. The same may be said of pain, and with equal reason. I can never persuade myself that pleasure and pain are mere relations, which can only exist as they are contrasted; but I think I can discern clearly that there are positive pains and pleasures, which do not at all depend upon each other. Nothing is more certain to my own feelings than this. There is nothing which I can distinguish in my mind with more clearness than the three states, of indifference, of pleasure, and of pain. Every one of these I can perceive without any sort of idea of its relation to anything else...

pleasure; pain; passion; indifference; feeling; the senses

Section XV, Of the effects of tragedy

...we shall be much mistaken if we attribute any considerable part of our satisfaction in tragedy to the consideration that tragedy is a deceit, and its representations no realities. The nearer it approaches the reality, and the further it removes us from all idea of fiction, the more perfect is its power. But be its power of what kind it will, it never approaches to what it represents. Choose a day on which to represent the most sublime and affecting tragedy we have; appoint the most favorite actors; spare no cost upon the scenes and decorations; unite the greatest efforts of poetry, painting, and music; and when you have collected your audience, just at the moment when their minds are erect with expectation, let it be reported that a state criminal of high rank is on the point of being executed in the adjoining square; in a moment the emptiness of the theatre would demonstrate the comparative weakness of the imitative arts, and proclaim the triumph of the real sympathy. I believe that this notion of our having a simple pain in the reality, yet a delight in the representation, arises from hence, that we do not sufficiently distinguish what we would by no means choose to do, from what we should be eager enough to see if it was once done...

tragedy; imitation; illusion; fiction; reality; representation; empathy; sympathy; aesthetics

Section XVI, Imitation

The second passion belonging to society is imitation, or, if you will, a desire of imitating, and consequently a pleasure in it. This passion arises from much the same cause with sympathy. For as sympathy makes us take a concern in whatever men feel, so this affection prompts us to copy whatever they do; and consequently we have a pleasure in imitating... It is by imitation far more than by precept, that we learn everything; and what we learn thus, we acquire not only more effectually, but more pleasantly...When the object represented in poetry or painting is such as we could have no desire of seeing in the reality, then I may be sure that its power in poetry or painting is owing to the power of imitation, and to no cause operating in the thing itself. So it is with most of the pieces which the painters call still-life. In these a cottage, a dung-hill, the meanest and most ordinary utensils of the kitchen, are capable of giving us pleasure. But when the object of the painting or poem is such as we should run to see if real, let it affect us with what odd sort of sense it will, we may rely upon it that the power of the poem or picture is more owing to the nature of the thing itself than to the mere effect of imitation, or to a consideration of the skill of the imitator, however excellent. Aristotle has spoken so much and so solidly upon the force of imitation in his Poetics, that it makes any further discourse upon this subject the less necessary.

imitation; desire; sympathy; pleasure; reality; instruction

Part V, Section IV, The effect of words

If words have all their possible extent of power, three effects arise in the mind of the hearer. The first is, the sound; the second, the picture, or representation of the thing signified by the sound; the third is, the affection of the soul produced by one or by both of the foregoing. Compounded abstract words, of which we have been speaking, (honor, justice, liberty, and the like,) produce the first and the last of these effects, but not the second. Simple abstracts are used to signify some one simple idea without much adverting to others which may chance to attend it, as blue, green, hot, cold, and the like; these are capable of affecting all three of the purposes of words; as the aggregate words, man, castle, horse, &c. are in a yet higher degree.

But I am of opinion, that the most general effect, even of these words, does not arise from their forming pictures of the several things they would represent in the imagination; because, on a very diligent examination of my own mind, and getting others to consider theirs, I do not find that once in twenty times any such picture is formed, and when it is, there is most commonly a particular effort of the imagination for that purpose. But the aggregate words operate, as I said of the compound-abstracts, not by presenting any image to the mind, but by having from use the same effect on being mentioned, that their original has when it is seen. Suppose we were to read a passage to this effect: "The river Danube rises in a moist and mountainous soil in the heart of Germany, where, winding to and fro, it waters several principalities, until, turning into Austria, and laving the walls of Vienna, it passes into Hungary; there with a vast flood, augmented by the Save and the Drave, it quits Christendom, and rolling through the barbarous countries which border on Tartary, it enters by many mouths in the Black Sea." In this description many things are mentioned, as mountains, rivers, cities, the sea, &c. But let anybody examine himself, and see whether he has had impressed on his imagination any pictures of a river, mountain, watery soil, Germany, &c. Indeed it is impossible, in the rapidity and quick succession of words in conversation, to have ideas both of the sound of the word, and of the thing represented; besides, some words, expressing real essences, are so mixed with others of a general and nominal import, that it is impracticable to jump from sense to thought, from particulars to generals, from things to words, in such a manner as to answer the purposes of life; nor is it necessary that we should.

emotion; sound; representation; meaning; reader-response; association; imagery; connotation; denotation; description

Section V, Examples that words may affect without raising images

...If I say, "I shall go to Italy next summer," I am well understood. Yet I believe nobody has by this painted in his imagination the exact figure of the speaker passing by land or by water, or both; sometimes on horseback, sometimes in a carriage: with all the particulars of the journey. Still less has he any idea of Italy, the country to which I proposed to go; or of the greenness of the fields, the ripening of the fruits, and the warmth of the air, with the change to this from a different season, which are the ideas for which the word summer is substituted; but least of all has he any image from the word next; for this word stands for the idea of many summers, with the exclusion of all but one: and surely the man who says next summer has no images of such a succession, and such an exclusion. In short, it is not only of those ideas which are commonly called abstract, and of which no image at all can be formed, but even of particular, real beings, that we converse without having any idea of them excited in the imagination; as will certainly appear on a diligent examination of our own minds. Indeed, so little does poetry depend for its effect on the power of raising sensible images, that I am convinced it would lose a very considerable part of its energy, if this were the necessary result of all description. Because that union of affecting words, which is the most powerful of all poetical instruments, would frequently lose its force along with its propriety and consistency, if the sensible images were always excited…In reality, poetry and rhetoric do not succeed in exact description so well as painting does; their business is, to affect rather by sympathy than imitation; to display rather the effect of things on the mind of the speaker, or of others, than to present a clear idea of the things themselves. This is their most extensive province, and that in which they succeed the best.

poetry; ideas; representation; meaning; imagination; abstract; language; images; evocation; reader-response

Section V1, Poetry not strictly an imitative art

Hence we may observe that poetry, taken in its most general sense, cannot with strict propriety be called an art of imitation. It is indeed an imitation so far as it describes the manners and passions of men which their words can express…But descriptive poetry operates chiefly by substitution; by the means of sounds, which by custom have the effect of realities. Nothing is an imitation further than as it resembles some other thing; and words undoubtedly have no sort of resemblance to the ideas for which they stand.

imitation; poetry; substitution; sounds; reality; ideas; words; semiology

Section V11, How words influence the passions

Now, as words affect, not by any original power, but by representation, it might be supposed, that their influence over the passions should be but light; yet it is quite otherwise; for we find by experience, that eloquence and poetry are as capable, nay indeed much more capable, of making deep and lively impressions than any other arts, and even than nature itself in very many cases. And this arises chiefly from these three causes. First, that we take an extraordinary part in the passions of others, and that we are easily affected and brought into sympathy by any tokens which are shown of them; and there are no tokens which can express all the circumstances of most passions so fully as words; so that if a person speaks upon any subject, he can not only convey the subject to you, but likewise the manner in which he is himself affected by it. Certain it is, that the influence of most things on our passions is not so much from the things themselves, as from our opinions concerning them; and these again depend very much on the opinions of other men, conveyable for the most part by words only. Secondly, there are many things of a very affecting nature, which can seldom occur in the reality, but the words that represent them often do; and thus they have an opportunity of making a deep impression and taking root in the mind, whilst the idea of the reality was transient; and to some perhaps never really occurred in any shape, to whom it is notwithstanding very affecting, as war, death, famine, &c...

Now, as there is a moving tone of voice, an impassioned countenance, an agitated gesture, which affect independently of the things about which they are exerted, so there are words, and certain dispositions of words, which being peculiarly devoted to passionate subjects, and always used by those who are under the influence of any passion, touch and move us more than those which far more clearly and distinctly express the subject-matter. We yield to sympathy what we refuse to description. The truth is, all verbal description, merely as naked description, though never so exact, conveys so poor and insufficient an idea of the thing described, that it could scarcely have the smallest effect, if the speaker did not call in to his aid those modes of speech that mark a strong and lively feeling in himself. Then, by the contagion of our passions, we catch a fire already kindled in another, which probably might never have been struck out by the object described.

representation; passions; sympathy; eloquence; language; poetry; reality; understanding; expression; empathy; point of view; emotion; reader-response

EDWARD YOUNG (1683–1765)

CONJECTURES ON ORIGINAL COMPOSITION *(1759)*

But there are, who write with vigor, and success, to the world's Delight, and their own Renown. These are the glorious fruits where Genius prevails. The mind of a man of Genius is a fertile and pleasant field, pleasant as *Elysium*...it enjoys a perpetual Spring. Of that Spring, *Originals* are the fairest Flowers: *Imitations* are of quicker growth, but fainter bloom. *Imitations* are of two kinds; one of Nature, one of Authors: The first we call *Originals*, and confine the term *Imitation* to the second. I shall not enter into the curious enquiry of what is, or is not, strictly speaking, *Original*, content with what all must allow, that some Compositions are more so than others; and the more they are so, I say, the better. *Originals* are, and ought to be, great Favourites, for they are great Benefactors; they extend the Republic of Letters, and add a new province to its dominion: *Imitators* only give us a sort of Duplicates of what we had, possibly much better, before; increasing the mere Drug of books, while all that makes them valuable, *Knowledge* and *Genius*, are at a stand. The pen of an *Original* Writer...out of a barren waste calls a blooming spring. Out of that blooming spring an *Imitator* is a transplanter of Laurels, which sometimes die on removal, always languish in a foreign soil...

An *Imitator* shares his crown, if he has one, with the chosen Object of his Imitation; an *Original* enjoys an undivided applause. An *Original* may be said to be of a *vegetable* nature; it rises spontaneously from the vital root of Genius; it *grows*, it is not *made*: *Imitations* are often a sort of *Manufacture*, wrought up by those *Mechanics*, *Art* and *Labour*, out of pre-existent materials not their own...

genius; originality; composition; imitation; knowledge; intertextuality

IMMANUEL KANT (1724–1804)

THE CRITIQUE OF JUDGEMENT *(1790)*
(translated by J. H. Bernard)

§ 1.
The judgement of taste is aesthetical

In order to decide whether anything is beautiful or not, we refer the representation, not by the Understanding to the Object for cognition but, by the Imagination (perhaps in conjunction with the Understanding) to the subject, and its feeling of pleasure or pain. The judgement of taste is therefore not a judgement of cognition, and is consequently not logical but aesthetical, by which we understand that whose determining ground can be no other than subjective. Every reference of representations, even that of sensations, may be objective (and then it signifies the real in an empirical representation); save only the reference to the feeling of pleasure and pain, by which nothing in the Object is signified, but through which there is a feeling in the subject, as it is affected by the representation.

To apprehend a regular, purposive building by means of one's cognitive faculty (whether in a clear or a confused way of representation) is something quite different from being conscious of this representation as connected with the sensation of satisfaction. Here the representation is altogether referred to the subject and to its feeling of life, under the name of the feeling of pleasure or pain. This establishes a quite separate faculty of distinction and of judgement, adding nothing to cognition, but only comparing the given representation in the subject with the whole faculty of representations, of which the mind is conscious in the feeling of its state. Given representations in a judgement can be empirical (consequently, aesthetical); but the judgement which is formed by means of them is logical, provided they are referred in the judgement to the Object. Conversely, if the given representations are rational, but are referred in a judgement simply to the subject (to its feeling), the judgement is so far always aesthetical.

§ 2.

The satisfaction which we combine with the representation of the existence of an object is called interest. Such satisfaction always has reference to the faculty of desire, either as its determining ground or as necessarily connected with its determining ground. Now when the question is if a thing is beautiful, we do not want to know whether anything depends or can depend on the existence of the thing either for myself or for any one else, but how we judge it by mere observation (intuition or reflection). If any one asks me if I find that palace beautiful which I see before me, I may answer: I do not like things of that kind which are made merely to be stared at.

…We wish only to know if this mere representation of the object is accompanied in me with satisfaction, however indifferent I may be as regards the existence of the object of this representation. We easily see that in saying it is beautiful and in showing that I have taste, I am concerned, not with that in which I depend on the existence of the object, but with that which I make out of this representation in myself. Every one must admit that a judgement about beauty, in which the least interest mingles, is very partial and is not a pure judgement of taste. We must not be in the least prejudiced in favour of the existence of the things, but be quite indifferent in this respect, in order to play the judge in things of taste.

§ 4.

Whatever by means of Reason pleases through the mere concept is good. That which pleases only as a means we call good for something (the useful); but that which pleases for itself is good in itself. In both there is always involved the concept of a purpose, and consequently the relation of Reason to the (at least possible) volition, and thus a satisfaction in the presence of an Object or an action, i.e. some kind of interest.

In order to find anything good, I must always know what sort of a thing the object ought to be, i.e. I must have a concept of it. But there is no need of this, to find a thing beautiful. Flowers, free delineations, outlines intertwined with one another without design and called foliage, have no meaning, depend on no definite concept, and yet they please. The satisfaction in the beautiful must depend on the reflection upon an object, leading to any concept (however indefinite); and it is thus distinguished from the pleasant which rests entirely upon sensation.

It is true, the Pleasant seems in many cases to be the same as the

Good. Thus people are accustomed to say that all gratification (especially if it lasts) is good in itself; which is very much the same as to say that lasting pleasure and the good are the same. But we can soon see that this is merely a confusion of words; for the concepts which properly belong to these expressions can in no way be interchanged. The pleasant, which, as such, represents the object simply in relation to Sense, must first be brought by the concept of a purpose under principles of Reason, in order to call it good, as an object of the Will. But that there is [involved] a quite different relation to satisfaction in calling that which gratifies at the same time good, may be seen from the fact that in the case of the good the question always is, whether it is mediately or immediately good (useful or good in itself); but on the contrary in the case of the pleasant there can be no question about this at all, for the word always signifies something which pleases immediately. (The same is applicable to what I call beautiful.)

Even in common speech men distinguish the Pleasant from the Good. Of a dish which stimulates the taste by spices and other condiments we say unhesitatingly that it is pleasant, though it is at the same time admitted not to be good; for though it immediately delights the senses, yet mediately, i.e. considered by Reason which looks to the after results, it displeases. Even in the judging of health we may notice this distinction. It is immediately pleasant to every one possessing it (at least negatively, i.e. as the absence of all bodily pains). But in order to say that it is good, it must be considered by Reason with reference to purposes; viz. that it is a state which makes us fit for all our business. Finally in respect of happiness every one believes himself entitled to describe the greatest sum of the pleasantnesses of life (as regards both their number and their duration) as a true, even as the highest, good. However, Reason is opposed to this. Pleasantness is enjoyment. And if we were concerned with this alone, it would be foolish to be scrupulous as regards the means which procure it for us, or [to care] whether it is obtained passively by the bounty of nature or by our own activity and work. But Reason can never be persuaded that the existence of a man who merely lives for enjoyment (however busy he may be in this point of view), has a worth in itself; even if he at the same time is conducive as a means to the best enjoyment of others, and shares in all their gratifications by sympathy. Only what he does, without reference to enjoyment, in full freedom and independently of what nature can procure for him passively, gives an [absolute] worth to his being, as the existence of a person; and happiness, with the whole abundance of its pleasures, is far from being an unconditioned good.

taste; aesthetics; beauty; imagination; cognition; pleasure; pain; subjective; objective value; judgement; interest; desire; reason; good; utility

MARY WOLLSTONECRAFT
(1759–1797)

A VINDICATION OF THE RIGHTS OF MEN
(1790)

It is a proverbial observation, that a very thin partition divides wit and madness. Poetry therefore naturally addresses the fancy, and the language of passion is with great felicity borrowed from the heightened picture which the imagination draws of sensible objects concentred by impassioned reflection. And, during this 'fine phrensy', reason has no right to rein-in the imagination, unless to prevent the introduction of supernumerary images; if the passion is real, the head will not be ransacked for stale tropes and cold rodomontade. I now speak of the genuine enthusiasm of genius, which, perhaps, seldom appears, but in the infancy of civilisation; for as this light becomes more luminous reason clips the wing of fancy – the youth becomes a man...

From observing several cold romantic characters I have been led to confine the term romantic to one definition – false, or rather artificial, feelings. Works of genius are read with a prepossession in their favour, and sentiments imitated, because they were fashionable and pretty, and not because they were forcibly felt.

In modern poetry the understanding and memory often fabricate the pretended effusions of the heart, and romance destroys all simplicity; which, in works of taste, is but a synonymous word for truth. This romantic spirit has extended to our prose, and scattered artificial flowers over the most barren heath; or a mixture of verse and prose producing the strangest incongruities. The turgid bombast of some of your periods fully proves these assertions; for when the heart speaks we are seldom shocked by hyperbole, or dry raptures...

Some celebrated writers have supposed that wit and judgement were incompatible; opposite qualities, that, in a kind of elementary strife, destroyed each other: and many men of wit have endeavoured to prove that they were mistaken. Much may be adduced by wits and metaphysicians on both sides of the question. But, from experience, I am apt to believe that they do weaken each other, and that great quickness of comprehension, and facile association of ideas, naturally preclude profundity of research. Wit is often a lucky hit; the result of a momentary inspiration. We know not whence it comes, and it blows where it lists. The operations of judgement, on the contrary, are cool and circumspect; and coolness and deliberation are great enemies to enthusiasm. If wit is of so fine a spirit, that it almost evaporates when translated into another language, why may not the temperature have an influence over it? This remark may be thought derogatory to the inferior qualities of the mind: but it is not a hasty one; and I mention it as a prelude to a conclusion I have frequently drawn, that the cultivation of reason damps fancy. The blessings of Heaven lie on each side; we must choose, if we wish to attain any degree of superiority, and not lose our lives in laborious idleness. If we mean to build our knowledge or happiness on a rational basis, we must learn to distinguish the *possible*, and not fight against the stream. And if we are careful to guard ourselves from imaginary sorrows and vain fears, we must also resign many enchanting illusions: for shallow must be the discernment which fails to discover that raptures and ecstasies arise from error. – Whether it will always be so, is not now to be discussed; suffice it to observe, that Truth is seldom arrayed by the Graces; and if she charms, it is only by inspiring a sober satisfaction, which takes its rise from a calm contemplation of proportion and simplicity. But, though it is allowed that one man has by nature more fancy than another, in each individual there is a spring-tide when fancy should govern and amalgamate materials for the understanding; and a graver period, when those materials should be employed by the judgement.

madness; poetry; fancy; imagination; reflection; genius; romantic; taste; judgement; truth; enthusiasm

A VINDICATION OF THE RIGHTS OF WOMAN *(1792)*

Chapter 111

…Women are every where in this deplorable state; for, in order to preserve their innocence, as ignorance is courteously termed, truth is hidden from them, and they are made to assume an artificial character before their faculties have acquired any strength. Taught from their infancy that beauty is woman's sceptre, the mind shapes itself to the body, and, roaming round its gilt cage, only seeks to adorn its prison. Men have various employments and pursuits which engage their attention, and give a character to the opening mind; but women, confined to one, and having their thoughts constantly directed to the most insignificant part of themselves, seldom extend their views beyond the triumph of the hour. But were their understanding once emancipated from the slavery to which the pride and sensuality of man and their short-sighted desire, like that of dominion in tyrants, of present sway, as subjected them, we should probably read of their weaknesses with surprise…

Chapter 1V

Novels, music, poetry, and gallantry, all tend to make women the creatures of sensation, and their character is thus formed in the mould of folly during the time they are acquiring accomplishments, the only improvement they are excited, by their station in society, to acquire. This overstretched sensibility naturally relaxes the other powers of the mind, and prevents intellect from attaining that sovereignty which it ought to attain to render a rational creature useful to others, and content with its own station: for the exercise of the understanding, as life advances, is the only method pointed out by nature to calm the passions…to their senses, women are made slaves, because it is by their sensibility that they obtain present power.

And will moralists pretend to assert, that this is the condition in which one half of the human race should be encouraged to remain with listless inactivity and stupid acquiescence? To remain, it may be said, innocent; they mean in a state of childhood. – We might as well never have been born, unless it were necessary that we should be created to enable man to acquire the noble privilege of reason, the power of discerning good from evil, whilst we lie down in the dust from whence we were taken, never to rise again.

It would be an endless task to trace the variety of meannesses, cares, and sorrows, into which women are plunged by the prevailing opinion, that they were created rather to feel than reason, and that all the power they obtain, must be obtained by their charms and weakness…

I am fully persuaded that we should hear of none of these infantine airs, if girls were allowed to take sufficient exercise, and not confined in close rooms till their muscles are relaxed, and their powers of digestion destroyed. To carry the remark still further, if fear in girls, instead of being cherished, perhaps, created, were treated in the same manner as cowardice in boys, we should quickly see women with more dignified aspects. It is true, they could not then with equal propriety be termed the sweet flowers that smile in the walk of man; but they would be more respectable members of society, and discharge the important duties of life by the light of their own reason. 'Educate women like men,' says Rousseau, 'and the more they resemble our sex the less power will they have over us.' This is the very point I aim at. I do not wish them to have power over men; but over themselves...

Chapter IX

Another instance of that feminine weakness of character, often produced by a confined education, is a romantic twist of the mind, which has been very properly termed *sentimental.*

Women subjected by ignorance to their sensations, and only taught to look for happiness in love, refine on sensual feelings, and adopt metaphysical notions respecting that passion, which lead them shamefully to neglect the duties of life, and frequently in the midst of these sublime refinements they plump into actual vice.

These are the women who are amused by the reveries of the stupid novelists, who, knowing little of human nature, work up stale tales, and describe meretricious scenes, all retailed in a sentimental jargon, which equally tend to corrupt the taste, and draw the heart aside from its daily duties...

Yet, when I exclaim against novels, I mean when contrasted with those works which exercise the understanding and regulate the imagination. – For any kind of reading I think better than leaving a blank still a blank, because the mind must receive a degree of enlargement and obtain a little strength by a slight exertion of its thinking powers; besides, even the productions that are only addressed to the imagination, raise the reader a little above the gross gratification of appetites, to which the mind has not given a shade of delicacy...

When, therefore, I advise my sex not to read such flimsy works, it is to induce them to read something superior; for I coincide in opinion with a sagacious man, who, having a daughter and niece under his care, pursued a very different plan with each.

The niece, who had considerable abilities, had, before she was left to his guardianship, been indulged in desultory reading. Her he endeavoured to lead, and did lead, to history and moral essays; but his daughter, whom a fond weak mother had indulged, and who consequently was averse to every thing like application, he allowed to read novels: and used to justify his conduct by saying, that if she ever attained a relish for reading them, he should have some foundation to work upon; and that erroneous opinions were better than none at all.

In fact the female mind has been so totally neglected, that knowledge was only to be acquired from this muddy source, till from reading novels some women of superior talents learned to despise them.

The best method, I believe, that can be adopted to correct a fondness for novels is to ridicule them: not indiscriminately, for then it would have little effect; but, if a judicious person, with some turn for humour, would read several to a young girl, and point out both by tones, and apt comparisons with pathetic incidents and heroic characters in history, how foolishly and ridiculously they caricatured human nature, just opinions might be substituted instead of romantic sentiments…

Besides, the reading of novels makes women, and particularly ladies of fashion, very fond of using strong expressions and superlatives in conversation; and, though the dissipated artificial life which they lead prevents their cherishing any strong legitimate passion, the language of passion in affected tones slips for ever from their glib tongues, and every trifle produces those phosphoric bursts which only mimick in the dark the flame of passion.

women; truth; gender; emancipation; intellect; senses; moralists; discrimination; education; equality; sentimental; reading; the novel

PART FOUR

Nineteenth Century

WILLIAM WORDSWORTH
(1772–1850)

ADVERTISEMENT TO THE LYRICAL BALLADS *(1798)*

The majority of the following poems are to be considered as experiments. They were written chiefly with a view to ascertain how far the language of conversation in the middle and lower classes of society is adapted to the purposes of poetic pleasure. Readers accustomed to the gaudiness and inane phraseology of many modern writers, if they persist in reading this book to its conclusion, will perhaps frequently have to struggle with feelings of strangeness and aukwardness: they will look round for poetry, and will be induced to enquire by what species of courtesy these attempts can be permitted to assume that title. It is desirable that such readers, for their own sakes, should not suffer the solitary word Poetry, a word of very disputed meaning, to stand in the way of their gratification; but that, while they are perusing this book, they should ask themselves if it contains a natural delineation of human passions, human characters, and human incidents; and if the answer be favourable to the author's wishes, that they should consent to be pleased in spite of that most dreadful enemy to our pleasures, our own pre-established codes of decision.

Readers of superior judgment may disapprove of the style in which many of these pieces are executed; it must be expected that many lines and phrases will not exactly suit their taste. It will perhaps appear to them, that wishing to avoid the prevalent fault of the day, the author has sometimes descended too low, and that many of his expressions are too familiar, and not of sufficient dignity. It is apprehended, that the more conversant the reader is with our elder writers, and with those in modern times who have been the most successful in painting manners and passions, the fewer complaints of this kind will he have to make.

An accurate taste in poetry, and in all the other arts, Sir Joshua Reynolds has observed, is an acquired talent, which can only be produced by severe thought, and a long continued intercourse with the best models of composition. This is mentioned not with so ridiculous a purpose as to prevent the most inexperienced reader from judging for himself; but merely to temper the rashness of decision, and to suggest that if poetry be a subject on which much time has not been bestowed, the judgment may be erroneous, and that in many cases it necessarily will be so.

poetry; subject matter; (ordinary) language; class; pleasure; style; taste; high/low art; intention; self-reflection

PREFACE TO THE EDITION OF 1800

Several of my Friends are anxious for the success of these Poems from a belief, that if the views, with which they were composed, were indeed realized, a class of Poetry would be produced, well adapted to interest mankind permanently, and not unimportant in the multiplicity and in the quality of its moral relations: and on this account they have advised me to prefix a systematic defence of the theory, upon which the poems were written. But I was unwilling to undertake the task, because I knew that on this occasion the Reader would look coldly upon my arguments, since I might be suspected of having been principally influenced by the selfish and foolish hope of *reasoning* him into an approbation of these particular Poems: and I was still more unwilling to undertake the task, because adequately to display my opinions and fully to enforce my arguments would require a space wholly disproportionate to the nature of a preface. For to treat the subject with the clearness and coherence, of which I believe it susceptible, it would be necessary to give a full account of the present state of the public taste in this country, and to determine how far this taste is healthy or depraved; which again could not be determined, without pointing out, in what manner language and the human mind act and react on each other, and without retracing the revolutions not of literature alone but likewise of society itself.

…The principal object then which I proposed to myself in these Poems was to make the incidents of common life interesting by tracing in them, truly though not ostentatiously, the primary laws of our nature: chiefly as far as regards the manner in which we associate ideas in a state of excitement.

Low and rustic life was generally chosen because in that situation the essential passions of the heart find a better soil in which they can attain their maturity, are less under restraint, and speak a plainer and more emphatic language; because in that situation our elementary feelings exist in a state of greater simplicity and consequently may be more accurately contemplated and more forcibly communicated; because the manners of rural life germinate from those elementary feelings; and from the necessary character of rural occupations are more easily comprehended; and are more durable; and lastly, because in that situation the passions of men are incorporated with the beautiful and permanent forms of nature. The language too of these men is adopted (purified indeed from what appear to be its real defects, from all lasting and rational causes of dislike or disgust) because such men hourly communicate with the best objects from which the best part of language is originally derived; and because, from their rank in society and the sameness and narrow circle of their intercourse, being less under the action of social vanity they convey their feelings and notions in simple and unelaborated expressions. Accordingly such a language arising out of repeated experience and regular feelings is a more permanent and a far more philosophical language than that which is frequently substituted for it by Poets, who think that they are conferring honour upon themselves and their art in proportion as they separate themselves from the sympathies of men, and indulge in arbitrary and capricious habits of expression in order to furnish food for fickle tastes and fickle appetites of their own creation...

...the Poems in these volumes will be found distinguished at least by one mark of difference, that each of them has a worthy *purpose*. Not that I mean to say, that I always began to write with a distinct purpose formally conceived; but I believe that my habits of meditation have so formed my feelings, as that my descriptions of such objects as strongly excite those feelings, will be found to carry along with them a *purpose*. If in this opinion I am mistaken I can have little right to the name of a Poet. For all good poetry is the spontaneous overflow of powerful feelings; but though this be true, Poems to which any value can be attached, were never produced on any variety of subjects but by a man who being possessed of more than usual organic sensibility had also thought long and deeply. For our continued influxes of feeling are modified and directed by our thoughts, which are indeed the representatives of all our past feelings; and as by contemplating the relation of these general representatives to each other, we discover what is really important to men, so by the repetition and continuance of this act feelings connected with important subjects will be nourished, till at length, if we be originally possessed of much organic sensibility, such habits of mind will be produced that by obeying blindly and mechanically the impulses of those habits we shall describe objects and utter sentiments of such a nature and in such connection with each other, that the understanding of the being to whom we address ourselves, if he be in a healthful state of association, must necessarily be in some degree enlightened, his taste exalted, and his affections ameliorated.

...Except in a very few instances the Reader will find no personifications of abstract ideas in these volumes, not that I mean to censure such personifications: they may be well fitted for certain sorts of composition, but in these Poems I propose to myself to imitate, and, as far as possible, to adopt the very language of men, and I do not find that such personifications make any regular or natural part of that language... There will also be found in these volumes little of what is usually called poetic diction; I have taken as much pains to avoid it as others ordinarily take to produce it; this I have done for the reason already alleged, to bring my language near to the language of men, and further, because the pleasure which I have proposed to myself to impart is of a kind very different from that which is supposed by many persons to be the proper object of poetry. I do not know how without being culpably particular I can give my Reader a more exact notion of the style in which I wished these poems to be written than by informing him that I have at all times endeavoured to look steadily at my subject, consequently I hope it will be found that there is in these Poems little falsehood of description, and that my ideas are expressed in language fitted to their respective importance.

If in a Poem there should be found a series of lines, or even a single line, in which the language, though naturally arranged and according to the strict laws of metre, does not differ from that of prose, there is a numerous class of critics who, when they stumble upon these prosaisms as they call them, imagine that they have made a notable discovery, and exult over the Poet as over a man ignorant of his own profession. Now these men would establish a canon of criticism which the Reader will conclude he must utterly reject if he wishes to be pleased with these volumes. And it would be a most easy task to prove to him that not only the language of a large portion of every good poem, even of the most elevated character, must necessarily, except with reference to the metre, in no respect differ from that of good prose, but likewise that some of the most interesting parts of the best poems will be found to be strictly the language of prose when prose is well written...

If it be affirmed that rhyme and metrical arrangement of themselves constitute a distinction which overturns what I have been saying on the strict affinity of metrical language with that of prose, and paves the way for other distinctions which the mind voluntarily admits, I answer that the distinction of rhyme and metre is regular and uniform, and not, like that which is produced by what is usually called poetic diction, arbitrary and subject to infinite caprices upon which no calculation whatever can be made. In the one case the Reader is utterly at the mercy of the Poet respecting what imagery or diction he may choose to connect with the passion, whereas in the other the metre obeys certain laws, to which the Poet and Reader both willingly submit because they are certain, and because no interference is made by them with the passion but such as the concurring testimony of ages has shewn to heighten and improve the pleasure which co-exists with it. It will now be proper to answer an obvious question, namely, why, professing these opinions have I written in verse? To this in the first place I reply, because, however I may have restricted myself, there is still left open to me what confessedly constitutes the most valuable object of all writing whether in prose or verse, the great and universal passions of men, the most general and interesting of their occupations, and the entire world of nature, from which I am at liberty to supply myself with endless combinations of forms and imagery.

…But I might point out various causes why, when the style is manly, and the subject of some importance, words metrically arranged will long continue to impart such a pleasure to mankind as he who is sensible of the extent of that pleasure will be desirous to impart. The end of Poetry is to produce excitement in coexistence with an overbalance of pleasure.

Now, by the supposition, excitement is an unusual and irregular state of the mind; ideas and feelings do not in that state succeed each other in accustomed order. But if the words by which this excitement is produced are in themselves powerful, or the images and feelings have an undue proportion of pain connected with them, there is some danger that the excitement may be carried beyond its proper bounds. Now the co-presence of something regular, something to which the mind has been accustomed when in an unexcited or a less excited state, cannot but have great efficacy in tempering and restraining the passion by an intertexture of ordinary feeling...

If I had undertaken a systematic defence of the theory upon which these poems are written, it would have been my duty to develop the various causes upon which the pleasure received from metrical language depends. Among the chief of these causes is to be reckoned a principle which must be well known to those who have made any of the Arts the object of accurate reflection; I mean the pleasure which the mind derives from the perception of similitude in dissimilitude. This principle is the great spring of the activity of our minds and their chief feeder. From this principle the direction of the sexual appetite, and all the passions connected with it take their origin: It is the life of our ordinary conversation; and upon the accuracy with which similitude in dissimilitude, and dissimilitude in similitude are perceived, depend our taste and our moral feelings...

I have said that Poetry is the spontaneous overflow of powerful feelings: it takes its origin from emotion recollected in tranquillity: the emotion is contemplated till by a species of reaction the tranquillity gradually disappears, and an emotion, similar to that which was before the subject of contemplation, is gradually produced, and does itself actually exist in the mind. In this mood successful composition generally begins, and in a mood similar to this it is carried on; but the emotion, of whatever kind and in whatever degree, from various causes is qualified by various pleasures, so that in describing any passions whatsoever, which are voluntarily described, the mind will upon the whole be in a state of enjoyment. Now if Nature be thus cautious in preserving in a state of enjoyment a being thus employed, the Poet ought to profit by the lesson thus held forth to him, and ought especially to take care, that whatever passions he communicates to his Reader, those passions, if his Reader's mind be sound and vigorous, should always be accompanied with an overbalance of pleasure. Now the music of harmonious metrical language, the sense of difficulty overcome, and the blind association of pleasure which has been previously received from works of rhyme or metre of the same or similar construction, all these imperceptibly make up a complex feeling of delight, which is of the most important use in tempering the painful feeling which will always be found intermingled with powerful descriptions of the deeper passions...

I have one request to make of my Reader, which is, that in judging these Poems he would decide by his own feelings genuinely, and not by reflection upon what will probably be the judgment of others. How common is it to hear a person say, "I myself do not object to this style of composition or this or that expression, but to such and such classes of people it will appear mean or ludicrous." This mode of criticism so destructive of all sound unadulterated judgment is almost universal: I have therefore to request that the Reader would abide independently by his own feelings, and that if he finds himself affected he would not suffer such conjectures to interfere with his pleasure...

...an *accurate* taste in Poetry and in all the other arts, as Sir

Joshua Reynolds has observed, is an *acquired* talent, which can only be produced by thought and a long continued intercourse with the best models of composition. This is mentioned not with so ridiculous a purpose as to prevent the most inexperienced Reader from judging for himself, (I have already said that I wish him to judge for himself;) but merely to temper the rashness of decision, and to suggest that if Poetry be a subject on which much time has not been bestowed, the judgment may be erroneous, and that in many cases it necessarily will be so…

From what has been said, and from a perusal of the Poems, the Reader will be able clearly to perceive the object which I have proposed to myself: he will determine how far I have attained this object; and, what is a much more important question, whether it be worth attaining; and upon the decision of these two questions will rest my claim to the approbation of the public.

universal; theory; taste; ordinary life; purpose; language; class; judgement; spontaneous overflow of powerful feelings; thought; style; rural life; abstract ideas; clichés; description; poetic diction; prose; poetry; metre; gender; pleasure; sexuality; similitude in dissimilitude; emotion recollected in tranquillity; particular/general; reader; triviality; reader-response

SAMUEL TAYLOR COLERIDGE (1772–1834)

BIOGRAPHIA LITERARIA *(1817)*

Chapter IV

…Repeated meditations led me first to suspect (and a more intimate analysis of the human faculties, their appropriate marks, functions and effects, matured my conjecture into full conviction), that fancy and imagination were two distinct and widely different faculties, instead of being, according to the general belief, either two names with one meaning, or at furthest the lower and higher degree of one and the same power…

fancy; imagination; faculties

Chapter XI

…With no other privilege than that of sympathy and sincere good wishes, I would address an affectionate exhortation to the youthful literati grounded on my own experience. It will be but short; for the beginning, middle and end converge to one charge: *never pursue literature as a trade*. With the exception of one extraordinary man I have never known an individual, least of all an individual of genius, healthy or happy without a profession, ie, some regular employment, which does not depend on the will of the moment, and which can be carried on so far mechanically that an average quantum only of health, spirits and intellectual exertion are requisite to its faithful discharge. Three hours of leisure, unannoyed by any alien anxiety and looked forward to with delight as a change and recreation, will suffice to realise in literature a larger product of what is truly genial than weeks of compulsion. Money and immediate reputation form only an arbitrary and accidental end of literary labor. The hope of increasing them by any given exertion will often prove a stimulant to industry; but the necessity of acquiring them will in all works of genius convert the stimulant into a narcotic. Motives by excess reverse their very nature, and instead of exciting stun and stupefy the mind. For it is one contradistinction of genius from talent, that its predominant end is always comprised in the means; and this is one of the many points which establish an analogy between genius and virtue. Now though talents may exist without genius, yet as genius cannot exist, certainly not manifest itself, without talents. I would advise every scholar who feels the genial power working within him so far to make a division between the two, as that he should devote his talents to the acquirement of competence in some known trade or profession...Then, when you retire into your study, in the books on your shelves you revisit so many venerable friends with whom you can converse...Even your writing desk with its blank paper and all its other implements will appear as a chain of flowers, capable of linking your feelings as well as thoughts to events and characters past or to come; not a chain of iron which binds you down to think of the future and the remote by recalling the claims and feelings of the peremptory present…

author; profession; genius; talent; trade; blank page

Chapter XIII

…The imagination then I consider either as primary, or secondary. The primary imagination I hold to be the living power and prime agent of all human perception, and as a repetition in the finite mind of the eternal act of creation in the infinite I AM. The secondary I consider as an echo of the former, co-existing with the conscious will, yet still as identical with the primary in the kind of its agency, and differing only in degree, and in the mode of its operation. It dissolves, diffuses, dissipates, in order to re-create; or where this process is rendered impossible, yet still, at all events, it struggles to idealise and to unify.

Fancy, on the contrary, has no other counters to play with but fixities and definites. The fancy is indeed no other than a mode of memory emancipated from the order of time and space; and blended with, and modified by that empirical phenomenon of the will which we express by the word *choice*. But equally with the ordinary memory it must receive all its materials ready made from the law of association…

imagination as primary; creativity; fancy; memory; self

JOHN KEATS (1795–1821)

Letters of John Keats, ed Forman, letter 90, Hampstead Sunday
[21 Dec. 1817]

...The excellence of every art is its intensity, capable of making all disagreeables evaporate, from their being in close relationship with Beauty and Truth...

I dined with Haydon the Sunday after you left, and had a very pleasant day, I dined too (for I have been out too much lately) with Horace Smith, and met his two Brothers, with Hill and Kingston, and one Du Bois. They only served to convince me, how superior humour is to wit in respect to enjoyment-These men say things which make one start, without making one feel; they are all alike; their manners are alike; they all know fashionables; they have a mannerism in their eating and drinking, in their mere handling a Decanter – They talked of Kean and his low company – Would I were with that Company instead of yours, said I to myself! I know such like acquaintance will never do for me and yet I am going to Reynolds on Wednesday. Brown and Dilke walked with me and back from the Christmas pantomime. I had not a dispute but a disquisition, with Dilke on various subjects; several things dove-tailed in my mind, and at once it struck me what quality went to form a Man of Achievement, especially in Literature, and which Shakespeare possessed so enormously – I mean Negative Capability, that is, when a man is capable of being in uncertainties, mysteries, doubts, without any irritable reaching after fact and reason-Coleridge, for instance, would let go by a fine isolated verisimilitude caught from the Penetralium of mystery, from being incapable of remaining content with half-knowledge. This pursued through volumes would perhaps take us no further than this, that with a great poet the sense of Beauty overcomes every other consideration, or rather obliterates all consideration.

John [Keats]

humour; wit; negative capability; doubt; knowledge; beauty; reason; fact; truth

THOMAS LOVE PEACOCK
(1785–1866)

THE FOUR AGES OF POETRY *(1820)*

The descriptive poetry of the present day has been called by its cultivators a return to nature. Nothing is more impertinent than this pretension. Poetry cannot travel out of the regions of its birth, the uncultivated lands of semi-civilized men. Mr. Wordsworth, the great leader of the returners to nature, cannot describe a scene under his own eyes without putting into it the shadow of a Danish boy or the living ghost of Lucy Gray, or some similar phantastical parturition of the moods of his own mind.

In the origin and perfection of poetry, all the associations of life were composed of poetical materials. With us it is decidedly the reverse. We know too that there are no Dryads in Hyde-park nor Naiads in the Regent's-canal. But barbaric manners and supernatural interventions are essential to poetry. Either in the scene, or in the time, or in both, it must be remote from our ordinary perceptions. While the historian and the philosopher are advancing in, and accelerating, the progress of knowledge, the poet is wallowing in the rubbish of departed ignorance, and raking up the ashes of dead savages to find gewgaws and rattles for the grown babies of the age. Mr. Scott digs up the poachers and cattle-stealers of the ancient border. Lord Byron cruizes for thieves and pirates on the shores of the Morea and among the Greek Islands…

These disjointed relics of tradition and fragments of second-hand observation, being woven into a tissue of verse, constructed on what Mr. Coleridge calls a new principle (that is, no principle at all), compose a modern-antique compound of frippery and barbarism, in which the puling sentimentality of the present time is grafted on the misrepresented ruggedness of the past into a heterogeneous congeries of unamalgamating manners, sufficient to impose on the common readers of poetry, over whose understandings the poet of this class possesses that commanding advantage, which, in all circumstances and conditions of life, a man who knows something, however little, always possesses over one who knows nothing.

A poet in our times is a semi-barbarian in a civilized community. He lives in the days that are past. His ideas, thoughts, feelings, associations, are all with barbarous manners, obsolete customs, and exploded superstitions. The march of his intellect is like that of a crab, backward. The brighter the light diffused around him by the progress of reason, the thicker is the darkness of antiquated barbarism, in which he buries himself like a mole, to throw up the barren hillocks of his Cimmerian labours. The philosophic mental tranquillity which looks round with an equal eye on all external things, collects a store of ideas, discriminates their relative value, assigns to all their proper place, and from the materials of useful knowledge thus collected, appreciated, and arranged, forms new combinations that impress the stamp of their power and utility on the real business of life, is diametrically the reverse of that frame of mind which poetry inspires, or from which poetry can emanate. The highest inspirations of poetry are resolvable into three ingredients: the rant of unregulated passion, the whining of exaggerated feeling, and the cant of factitious sentiment…It can never make a philosopher, nor a statesman, nor in any class of life an useful or rational man. It cannot claim the slightest share in any one of the comforts and utilities of life of which we have witnessed so many and so rapid advances. But though not useful, it may be said it is highly ornamental, and deserves to be cultivated for the pleasure it yields. Even if this be granted, it does not follow that a writer of poetry in the present state of society is not a waster of his own time, and a robber of that of others. Poetry is not one of those arts which, like painting, require repetition and multiplication, in order to be diffused among society. There are more good poems already existing than are sufficient to employ that portion of life which any mere reader and recipient of poetical impressions should devote to them, and these having been produced in poetical times, are far superior in all the characteristics of poetry to the artificial reconstructions of a few morbid ascetics in unpoetical times. To read the promiscuous rubbish of the present time to the exclusion of the select treasures of the past, is to substitute the worse for the better variety of the same mode of enjoyment…

…when we consider that the great and permanent interests of human society become more and more the main spring of intellectual pursuit; that in proportion as they become so, the subordinacy of the ornamental to the useful will be more and more seen and acknowledged; and that therefore the progress of useful art and science, and of moral and political knowledge, will continue more and more to withdraw attention from frivolous and unconducive, to solid and conducive studies:

that therefore the poetical audience will not only continually diminish in the proportion of its number to that of the rest of the reading public, but will also sink lower and lower in the comparison of intellectual acquirement: when we consider that the poet must still please his audience, and must therefore continue to sink to their level, while the rest of the community is rising above it: we may easily conceive that the day is not distant, when the degraded state of every species of poetry will be as generally recognized as that of dramatic poetry has long been: and this not from any decrease either of intellectual power, or intellectual acquisition, but because intellectual power and intellectual acquisition have turned themselves into other and better channels, and have abandoned the cultivation and the fate of poetry to the degenerate fry of modern rhymesters, and their olympic judges, the magazine critics, who continue to debate and promulgate oracles about poetry, as if it were still what it was in the Homeric age, the all-in-all of intellectual progression, and as if there were no such things in existence as mathematicians, astronomers, chemists, moralists, metaphysicians, historians, politicians, and political economists…

imitation; authority; realism; clichés; genius; memory; reason; supernatural; sentimentality; poetry as moribund; ethics; ego; poet as barbarian

PERCY BYSSHE SHELLEY
(1792–1822)

A DEFENCE OF POETRY *(1840)*

According to one mode of regarding those two classes of mental action, which are called reason and imagination, the former may be considered as mind contemplating the relations borne by one thought to another, however produced; and the latter, as mind acting upon those thoughts so as to colour them with its own light, and composing from them, as from elements, other thoughts, each containing within itself the principle of its own integrity. The one is the...principle of synthesis, and has for its objects those forms which are common to universal nature and existence itself; the other is the...principle of analysis, and its action regards the relations of things, simply as relations; considering thoughts, not in their integral unity, but as the algebraical representations which conduct to certain general results. Reason is the enumeration of quantities already known; imagination is the perception of the value of those quantities, both separately and as a whole. Reason respects the differences, and imagination the similitudes of things. Reason is to the imagination as the instrument to the agent, as the body to the spirit, as the shadow to the substance.

Poetry, in a general sense, may be defined to be 'the expression of the imagination': and poetry is connate with the origin of man. Man is an instrument over which a series of external and internal impressions are driven, like the alternations of an ever-changing wind over an Aeolian lyre, which move it by their motion to ever-changing melody...

Every man in the infancy of art observes an order which approximates more or less closely to that from which this highest delight results: but the diversity is not sufficiently marked, as that its gradations should be sensible, except in those instances where the predominance of this faculty of approximation to the beautiful (for so we may be permitted to name the relation between this highest pleasure and its cause) is very great. Those in whom it exists in excess are poets, in the most universal sense of the word; and the pleasure resulting from the manner in which they express the influence of society or nature upon their own minds, communicates itself to others, and gathers a sort of reduplication from that community. Their language is vitally metaphorical; that is, it marks the before unapprehended relations of things and perpetuates their apprehension, until the words which represent them become, through time, signs for portions or classes of thoughts instead of pictures of integral thoughts; and then if no new poets should arise to create afresh the associations which have been thus disorganized, language will be dead to all the nobler purposes of human intercourse...

In the infancy of society every author is necessarily a poet, because language itself is poetry; and to be a poet is to apprehend the true and the beautiful, in a word, the good which exists in the relation, subsisting, first between existence and perception, and secondly between perception and expression. Every original language near to its source is in itself the chaos of a cyclic poem: the copiousness of lexicography and the distinctions of grammar are the works of a later age, and are merely the catalogue and the form of the creations of poetry.

But poets, or those who imagine and express this indestructible order, are not only the authors of language and of music, of the dance, and architecture, and statuary, and painting; they are the institutors of laws, and the founders of civil society, and the inventors of the arts of life, and the teachers, who draw into a certain propinquity with the beautiful and the true, that partial apprehension of the agencies of the invisible world which is called religion. Hence all original religions are allegorical, or susceptible of allegory, and, like Janus, have a double face of false and true. Poets, according to the circumstances of the age and nation in which they appeared, were called, in the earlier epochs of the world, legislators, or prophets: a poet essentially comprises and unites both these characters. For he not only beholds intensely the present as it is, and discovers those laws according to which present things ought to be ordered, but he beholds the future in the present, and his thoughts are the germs of the flower and the fruit of latest time. Not that I assert poets to be prophets in the gross sense of the word, or that they can foretell the form as surely as they foreknow the spirit of events: such is the pretence of superstition, which would make poetry an attribute of prophecy, rather than prophecy an attribute of poetry, colour, form, and religious and civil habits of action, are all the instruments and materials of poetry; they may be called poetry by that figure of speech which considers the effect as a synonym of the cause. But poetry in a more restricted sense expresses those arrangements of language, and especially metrical language, which are created by that imperial faculty; whose throne is curtained within the invisible nature of man.

And this springs from the nature itself of language, which is a more direct representation of the actions and passions of our internal being, and is susceptible of more various and delicate combinations, than colour, form, or motion, and is more plastic and obedient to the control of that faculty of which it is the creation. For language is arbitrarily produced by the imagination and has relation to thoughts alone; but all other materials, instruments and conditions of art, have relations among each other, which limit and interpose between conception and expression The former is as a mirror which reflects, the latter as a cloud which enfeebles, the light of which both are mediums of communication. Hence the fame of sculptors, painters, and musicians, although the intrinsic powers of the great masters of these arts may yield in no degree to that of those who have employed language as the hieroglyphic of their thoughts, has never equalled that of poets in the restricted sense of the term, as two performers of equal skill will produce unequal effects from a guitar and a harp.

...An observation of the regular mode of the recurrence of harmony in the language of poetical minds, together with its relation to music, produced metre, or a certain system of traditional forms of harmony and language. Yet it is by no means essential that a poet should accommodate his language to this traditional form, so that the harmony, which is its spirit, be observed. The practice is indeed convenient and popular, and to be preferred, especially in such composition as includes much action: but every great poet must inevitably innovate upon the example of his predecessors in the exact structure of his peculiar versification. The distinction between poets and prose writers is a vulgar error. The distinction between philosophers and poets has been anticipated. Plato was essentially a poet--

the truth and splendour of his imagery, and the melody of his language, are the most intense that it is possible to conceive. He rejected the measure of the epic, dramatic, and lyrical forms, because he sought to kindle a harmony in thoughts divested of shape and action, and he forbore to invent any regular plan of rhythm which would include, under determinate forms, the varied pauses of his style…

A poem is the very image of life expressed in its eternal truth. There is this difference between a story and a poem, that a story is a catalogue of detached facts, which have no other connexion than time, place, circumstance, cause and effect; the other is the creation of actions according to the unchangeable forms of human nature, as existing in the mind of the Creator, which is itself the image of all other minds. The one is partial, and applies only to a definite period of time, and a certain combination of events which can never again recur; the other is universal, and contains within itself the germ of a relation to whatever motives or actions have place in the possible varieties of human nature. Time, which destroys the beauty and the use of the story of particular facts, stripped of the poetry which should invest them, augments that of poetry, and for ever develops new and wonderful applications of the eternal truth which it contains. Hence epitomes have been called the moths of just history; they eat out the poetry of it. A story of particular facts is as a mirror which obscures and distorts that which should be beautiful: poetry is a mirror which makes beautiful that which is distorted…

Poetry is ever accompanied with pleasure: all spirits on which it falls open themselves to receive the wisdom which is mingled with its delight…A poet is a nightingale, who sits in darkness and sings to cheer its own solitude with sweet sounds;

his auditors are as men entranced by the melody of an unseen musician, who feel that they are moved and softened, yet know not whence or why...

...Poetry lifts the veil from the hidden beauty of the world, and makes familiar objects be as if they were not familiar; it reproduces all that it represents, and the impersonations clothed in its Elysian light stand thenceforward in the minds of those who have once contemplated them as memorials of that gentle and exalted content which extends itself over all thoughts and actions with which it coexists. The great secret of morals is love; or a going out of our own nature, and an identification of ourselves with the beautiful which exists in thought, action, or person, not our own. A man, to be greatly good, must imagine intensely and comprehensively; he must put himself in the place of another and of many others; the pains and pleasures of his species must become his own. The great instrument of moral good is the imagination; and poetry administers to the effect by acting upon the cause. Poetry enlarges the circumference of the imagination by replenishing it with thought of ever new delight, which have the power of attracting and assimilating to their own nature all other thoughts, and which form new intervals and interstices whose void for ever craves fresh food. Poetry strengthens the faculty which is the organ of the moral nature of man, in the same manner as exercise strengthens a limb...

The drama being that form under which a greater number of modes of expression of poetry are susceptible of being combined than any other, the connexion of poetry and social good is more observable in the drama than in whatever other form. And it is indisputable that the highest perfection of human society has ever corresponded with the highest dramatic excellence; and that the corruption or the extinction of the drama in a nation where it has once flourished, is a mark of a corruption of manners and an extinction of the energies which sustain the soul of social life. But, as Machiavelli says of political institutions, that life may be preserved and renewed, if men should arise capable of bringing back the drama to its principles. And this is true with respect to poetry in its most extended sense: all language, institution and form, require not only to be produced but to be sustained: the office and character of a poet participates in the divine nature as regards providence, no less than as regards creation…

It is admitted that the exercise of the imagination is most delightful, but it is alleged that that of reason is more useful. Let us examine as the grounds of this distinction, what is here meant by utility. Pleasure or good, in a general sense, is that which the consciousness of a sensitive and intelligent being seeks, and in which, when found, it acquiesces. There are two kinds of pleasure, one durable, universal and permanent; the other transitory and particular. Utility may either express the means of producing the former or the latter. In the former sense, whatever strengthens and purifies the affections, enlarges the imagination, and adds spirit to sense, is useful. But a narrower meaning may be assigned to the word utility, confining it to express that which banishes the importunity of the wants of our animal nature, the surrounding men with security of life, the dispersing the grosser delusions of superstition, and the conciliating such a degree of mutual forbearance among men as may consist with the motives of personal advantage.

We want the creative faculty to imagine that which we know; we want the generous impulse to act that which we imagine; we want the poetry of life: our calculations have outrun conception; we have eaten more than we can digest. The cultivation of those sciences which have enlarged the limits of the empire of man over the external world, has, for want of the poetical faculty, proportionally circumscribed those of the internal world; and man, having enslaved the elements, remains himself a slave. To what but a cultivation of the mechanical arts in a degree disproportioned to the presence of the creative faculty, which is the basis of all knowledge, is to be attributed the abuse of all invention for abridging and combining labour, to the exasperation of the inequality of mankind?...Poetry, and the principle of Self, of which money is the visible, incarnation, are the God and Mammon of the world...

Poetry is indeed something divine. It is at once the centre and circumference of knowledge; it is that which comprehends all science, and that to which all science must be referred. It is at the same time the root and blossom of all other systems of thought; it is that from which all spring, and that which adorns all; and that which, if blighted, denies the fruit and the seed, and withholds from the barren world the nourishment and the succession of the scions of the tree of life. It is the perfect and consummate surface and bloom of all things; it is as the odour and the colour of the rose to the texture of the elements which compose it, as the form and splendour of unfaded beauty to the secrets of anatomy and corruption. What were virtue, love, patriotism, friendship—what were the scenery of this beautiful universe which we inhabit; what were our consolations on this side of the grave—and what were our aspirations beyond it, if poetry did not ascend to bring light and fire from those eternal regions where the owl-winged faculty of calculation dare not ever soar? Poetry is not like reasoning, a power to be exerted according to the determination of the will. A man cannot say, 'I will compose poetry.' The greatest poet even cannot say it; for the mind in creation is as a fading coal, which some invisible influence, like an inconstant wind, awakens to transitory brightness; this power arises from within, like the colour of a flower which fades and changes as it is developed, and the conscious portions of our natures are unprophetic either of its approach or its departure. Could this influence be durable in its original purity and force, it is impossible to predict the greatness of the results; but when composition begins, inspiration is already on the decline, and the most glorious poetry that has ever been communicated to the world is probably a feeble shadow of the original conceptions of the poet. I appeal to the greatest poets of the present day, whether it is not an error to assert that the finest passages of poetry are produced by labour and study. The toil and the delay recommended by critics, can be justly interpreted to mean no more than a careful observation of the inspired moments, and an artificial connexion of the spaces between their suggestions by the intertexture of conventional expressions; a necessity only imposed by the limitedness of the poetical faculty itself; for Milton conceived the Paradise Lost as a whole before he executed it in portions; We have his own authority also for the muse having 'dictated' to him the 'unpremeditated song'…

Poetry is the record of the best and happiest moments of the happiest and best minds. We are aware of evanescent visitations of thought and feeling sometimes associated with place or person, sometimes regarding our own mind alone, and always arising unforeseen and departing unbidden, but elevating and delightful beyond all expression; so that even in the desire and regret they leave, there cannot but be pleasure, participating as it does in the nature of its object. It is as it were the interpenetration of a diviner nature through our own; but its footsteps are like those of a wind over the sea, which the coming calm erases, and whose traces remain only, as on the wrinkled sand which paves it. These and corresponding conditions of being are experienced principally by those of the most delicate sensibility and the most enlarged imagination; and the state of mind produced by them is at war with every base desire. The enthusiasm of virtue, love, patriotism, and friendship, is essentially linked with such emotions; and whilst they last, self appears as what it is, an atom to a universe.

...Poetry turns all things to loveliness; it exalts the beauty of that which is most beautiful, and it adds beauty to that which is most deformed; it marries exultation and horror, grief and pleasure, eternity and change; it subdues to union under its light yoke, all irreconcilable things. It transmutes all that it touches, and every form moving within the radiance of its presence is changed by wondrous sympathy to an incarnation of the spirit which it breathes: its secret alchemy turns to potable gold the poisonous waters which flow from death through life; it strips the veil of familiarity from the world, and lays bare the naked and sleeping beauty, which is the spirit of its forms...

Poetry, as has been said, differs in this respect from logic, that it is not subject to the control of the active powers of the mind, and that its birth and recurrence have no necessary connexion with the consciousness or will. It is presumptuous to determine that these are the necessary conditions of all mental causation, when mental effects are experienced unsusceptible of being referred to them. The frequent recurrence of the poetical power, it is obvious to suppose, may produce in the mind a habit of order and harmony correlative with its own nature and its effects upon other minds. But in the intervals of inspiration, and they may be frequent without being durable, a poet becomes a man, and is abandoned to the sudden reflux of the influences under which others habitually live. But as he is more delicately organized than other men, and sensible to pain and pleasure, both his own and that of others, in a degree unknown to them, he will avoid the one and pursue the other with an ardour proportioned to this difference...

...the literature of England, an energetic development of which has ever preceded or accompanied a great and free development of the national will, has arisen as it were from a new birth. In spite of the low-thoughted envy which would undervalue contemporary merit, our own will be a memorable age in intellectual achievements, and we live among such philosophers and poets as surpass beyond comparison any who have appeared since the last national struggle for civil and religious liberty. The most unfailing herald, companion, and follower of the awakening of a great people to work a beneficial change in opinion or institution, is poetry. At such periods there is an accumulation of the power of communicating and receiving intense and impassioned conceptions respecting man and nature. The persons in whom this power resides may often, as far as regards many portions of their nature, have little apparent correspondence with that spirit of good of which they are the ministers. But even whilst they deny and abjure, they are yet compelled to serve, the power which is seated on the throne of their own soul. It is impossible to read the compositions of the most celebrated writers of the present day without being startled with the electric life which burns within their words. They measure the circumference and sound the depths of human nature with a comprehensive and all-penetrating spirit, and they are themselves perhaps the most sincerely astonished at its manifestations; for it is less their spirit than the spirit of the age. Poets are the hierophants of an unapprehended inspiration; the mirrors of the gigantic shadows which futurity casts upon the present; the words which express what they understand not; the trumpets which sing to battle, and feel not what they inspire; the influence which is moved not, but moves. Poets are the unacknowledged legislators of the world.

reason; imagination; synthesis; poetry; passions; pleasure; rhythm; harmony; mimetic representation; taste; beauty; metaphor; language; truth; poets; existence; perception; expression; grammar; religion; allegory; legislators; morality; prophets; eternal; infinite; metaphor; translation; prose; philosophers; style; story; composition; tragedy; love; consciousness; judgement; character; ambition; identification; morality; science; ethics; cause and effect; tragedy; self-knowledge; drama; gender; past; intertextuality; self; sexuality; inspiration; labour; study; pain; muse; criticism; logic; reason; utility; pleasure; the divine; poets as unacknowledged legislators of the world

EDGAR ALLAN POE
(1809–1849)

(review of 'Twice-Told Tales', by Nathaniel Hawthorne; Graham's Magazine, April, 1842

The tale proper, in our opinion, affords unquestionably the fairest field for the exercise of the loftiest talent, which can be afforded by the wide domains of mere prose. Were we bidden to say how the highest genius could be most advantageously employed for the best display of its own powers, we should answer, without hesitation — in the composition of a rhymed poem, not to exceed in length what might be perused in an hour. Within this limit alone can the highest order of true poetry exist. We need only here say, upon this topic, that, in almost all classes of composition, the unity of effect or impression is a point of the greatest importance. It is clear, moreover, that this unity cannot be thoroughly preserved in productions whose perusal cannot be completed at one sitting. We may continue the reading of a prose composition, from the very nature of prose itself, much longer than we can persevere, to any good purpose, in the perusal of a poem. This latter, if truly fulfilling the demands of the poetic sentiment, induces an exaltation of the soul which cannot be long sustained. All high excitements are necessarily transient. Thus a long poem is a paradox. And, without unity of impression, the deepest effects cannot be brought about. Epics were the Spring of an imperfect sense of Art, and their reign is no more. A poem too brief may produce a vivid, but never an intense or enduring impression. Without a certain continuity of effort — without a certain duration or repetition of purpose — the soul is never deeply moved...Extreme brevity will degenerate into epigrammatism; but the sin of extreme length is even more unpardonable. *In medio tutissimus ibis.*

Were we called upon however to designate that class of composition which, next to such a poem as we have suggested, should best fulfil the demands of high genius — should offer it the most advantageous field of exertion — we should unhesitatingly speak of the prose tale, as Mr. Hawthorne has here exemplified it. We allude to the short prose narrative, requiring from a half-hour to one or two hours in its perusal. The ordinary novel is objectionable, from its length, for reasons already stated in substance. As it cannot be read at one sitting, it deprives itself, of course, of the immense force derivable from totality. Worldly interests intervening during the pauses of perusal, modify, annul, or counteract, in a greater or less degree, the impressions of the book. But simple cessation in reading would, of itself, be sufficient to destroy the true unity. In the brief tale, however, the author is enabled to carry out the fulness of his intention, be it what it may. During the hour of perusal the soul of the reader is at the writer's control. There are no external or extrinsic influences — resulting from weariness or interruption.

A skilful literary artist has constructed a tale. If wise, he has not fashioned his thoughts to accommodate his incidents;

but having conceived, with deliberate care, a certain unique or single effect to be wrought out, he then invents such incidents — he then combines such events as may best aid him in establishing this preconceived effect. If his very initial sentence tend not to the outbringing of this effect, then he has failed in his first step. In the whole composition there should be no word written, of which the tendency, direct or indirect, is not to the one pre-established design. And by such means, with such care and skill, a picture is at length painted which leaves in the mind of him who contemplates it with a kindred art, a sense of the fullest satisfaction. The idea of the tale has been presented unblemished, because undisturbed; and this is an end unattainable by the novel. Undue brevity is just as exceptionable here as in the poem; but undue length is yet more to be avoided.

We have said that the tale has a point of superiority even over the poem. In fact, while the rhythm of this latter is an essential aid in the development of the poem's highest idea — the idea of the Beautiful — the artificialities of this rhythm are an inseparable bar to the development of all points of thought or expression which have their basis in Truth. But Truth is often, and in very great degree, the aim of the tale. Some of the finest tales are tales of ratiocination. Thus the field of this species of composition, if not in so elevated a region on the mountain of Mind, is a table-land of far vaster extent than the domain of the mere poem. Its products are never so rich, but infinitely more numerous, and more appreciable by the mass of mankind. The writer of the prose tale, in short, may bring to his theme a vast variety of modes or inflections of thought and expression — (the ratiocinative, for example, the sarcastic or the humorous) which are not only antagonistical to the nature of the poem, but absolutely forbidden by one of its most peculiar and indispensable adjuncts; we allude of course, to rhythm. It may be added, here, par parentheses, that the author who aims at the purely beautiful in a prose tale is laboring at great disadvantage. For Beauty can be better treated in the poem. Not so with terror, or passion, or horror, or a multitude of such other points.

short story; tale; prose fiction; genius; unity of effect; epic; soul; novel; reader; structure; the beautiful; truth; mind; terror; passion

JOHN RUSKIN (1819–1900)

OF THE PATHETIC FALLACY *(1856)*

§ 1. GERMAN dulness, and English affectation, have of late much multiplied among us the use of two of the most objectionable words that were ever coined by the troublesomeness of metaphysicians — namely, 'Objective' and 'Subjective'…

The word 'Blue', say certain philosophers, means the sensation of colour which the human eye receives in looking at the open sky, or at a bell gentian.

Now, say they farther, as this sensation can only be felt when the eye is turned to the object, and as, therefore, no such sensation is produced by the object when nobody looks at it, therefore the thing, when it is not looked at, is not blue; and thus (say they) there are many qualities of things which depend as much on something else as on themselves. To be sweet, a thing must have a taster; it is only sweet while it is being tasted, and if the tongue had not the capacity of taste, then the sugar would not have the quality of sweetness.

And then they agree that the qualities of things which thus depend upon our perception of them, and upon our human nature as affected by them, shall be called Subjective; and the qualities of things which they always have, irrespective of any other nature, as roundness or squareness, shall be called Objective...

§ 2. Now, to get rid of all these ambiguities and troublesome words at once, be it observed that the word ‹Blue› does not mean the sensation caused by a gentian on the human eye; but it means the power of producing that sensation; and this power is always there, in the thing, whether we are there to experience it or not, and would remain there though there were not left a man on the face of the earth. Precisely in the same way gunpowder has a power of exploding. It will not explode if you put no match to it. But it has always the power of so exploding, and is therefore called an explosive compound, which it very positively and assuredly is, whatever philosophy may say to the contrary...

§ 3. Hence I would say to these philosophers: If, instead of using the sonorous phrase, ‹It is objectively so,› you will use the plain old phrase, ‹It is so ;› and if instead of the sonorous phrase, ‹It is subjectively so,› you will say, in plain old English, ‹It does so,› or ‹It seems so to me;› you will, on the whole, be more intelligible to your fellow-creatures...If you find that you cannot explode the gunpowder, you will not declare that all gunpowder is subjective, and all explosion imaginary, but you will simply suspect and declare yourself to be an ill-made match...

§ 4. Now, therefore, putting these tiresome and absurd words quite out of our way, we may go on at our ease to examine the point in question—namely, the difference between the ordinary, proper, and true appearances of things to us; and the extraordinary, or false appearances, when we are under the influence of emotion, or contemplative fancy; false appearances, I say, as being entirely unconnected with any real power or character in the object, and only imputed to it by us.

For instance —

The spendthrift crocus, bursting through the mould
Naked and shivering, with his cup of gold.

This is very beautiful, and yet very untrue. The crocus is not a spendthrift, but a hardy plant; its yellow is not gold, but saffron. How is it that we enjoy so much the having it put into our heads that it is anything else than a plain crocus?

It is an important question. For, throughout our past reasonings about art, we have always found that nothing could be good, or useful, or ultimately pleasurable, which was untrue. But here is something pleasurable in written poetry which is nevertheless untrue. And what is more, if we think over our favourite poetry, we shall find it full of this kind of fallacy, and that we like it all the more for being so.

§ 5. It will appear also, on consideration of the matter, that this fallacy is of two principal kinds. Either, as in this case of the crocus, it is the fallacy of wilful fancy, which involves no real expectation that it will be believed; or else it is a fallacy caused by an excited state of the feelings, making us, for the time, more or less irrational. Of the cheating of the fancy we shall have to speak presently; but, in this chapter, I want to examine the nature of the other error, that which the mind admits when affected strongly by emotion. Thus, for instance, in Alton Locke—

They rowed her in across the rolling foam—
The cruel, crawling foam.

The foam is not cruel, neither does it crawl. The state of mind which attributes to it these characters of a living creature is one in which the reason is unhinged by grief. All violent feelings have the same effect. They produce in us a falseness in all our impressions of external things, which I would generally characterize as the 'Pathetic Fallacy'.

§ 6. Now we are in the habit of considering this fallacy as eminently a character of poetical description, and the temper of mind in which we allow it as one eminently poetical, because passionate. But, I believe, if we look well into the matter, that we shall find the greatest poets do not often admit this kind of falseness — that it is only the second order of poets who much delight in it...

§ 8. The temperament which admits the pathetic fallacy, is, as I said above, that of a mind and body in some sort too weak to deal fully with what is before them or upon them; borne away, or over-clouded, or over-dazzled by emotion; and it is a more or less noble state, according to the force of the emotion which has induced it. For it is no credit to a man that he is not morbid or inaccurate in his perceptions, when he has no strength of feeling to warp them; and it is in general a sign of higher capacity and stand in the ranks of being, that the emotions should be strong enough to vanquish, partly, the intellect, and make it believe what they choose. But it is still a grander condition when the intellect also rises, till it is strong enough to assert its rule against, or together with, the utmost efforts of the passions; and the whole man stands in an iron glow, white hot, perhaps, but still strong, and in no wise evaporating; even if he melts, losing none of his weight.

So, then, we have the three ranks: the man who perceives rightly, because he does not feel, and to whom the primrose is very accurately the primrose, because he does not love it. Then, secondly, the man who perceives wrongly, because he feels, and to whom the primrose is anything else than a primrose: a star, or a sun, or a fairy's shield, or a forsaken maiden. And then, lastly, there is the man who perceives rightly in spite of his feelings, and to whom the primrose is for ever nothing else than itself—a little flower, apprehended in the very plain and leafy fact of it, whatever and how many soever the associations and passions may be, that crowd around it. And, in general, these three classes may be rated in comparative order, as the men who are not poets at all, and the poets of the second order, and the poets of the first; only however great a man may be, there are always some subjects which ought to throw him off his balance; some, by which his poor human capacity of thought should be conquered, and brought into the inaccurate and vague state of perception, so that the language of the highest inspiration becomes broken, obscure, and wild in metaphor, resembling that of the weaker man, overborne by weaker things.

§ 9. And thus, in full, there are four classes: the men who feel nothing, and therefore see truly; the men who feel strongly, think weakly, and see untruly (second order of poets); the men who feel strongly, think strongly, and see truly (first order of poets); and the men who, strong as human creatures can be, are yet submitted to influences stronger than they, and see in a sort untruly, because what they see is inconceivably above them. This last is the usual condition of prophetic inspiration.

objective; subjective; sense; response; reality; illusion; truth; close reading; useful; Pathetic Fallacy; intellect; prose; gender

ELIZABETH BARRETT BROWNING (1806–1861)

AURORA LEIGH *(1857)*

THIRD BOOK

I worked on, on.
Through all the bristling fence of nights and days
Which hedges time in from the eternities,
I struggled… never stopped to note the stakes
Which hurt me in my course. The midnight oil
Would stink sometimes; there came some vulgar needs:
I had to live, that therefore I might work.
And, being but poor, I was constrained, for life,
To work with one hand for the booksellers,
While working with the other for myself
And art. You swim with feet as well as hands
Or make small way. I apprehended this,–
In England, no one lives by verse that lives;
And, apprehending, I resolved by prose
To make a space to sphere my living verse.
I wrote for cyclopædias, magazines,

And weekly papers, holding up my name
To keep it from the mud. I learnt the use
Of the editorial 'we' in a review,
As courtly ladies the fine trick of trains,
And swept it grandly through the open doors
As if one could not pass through doors at all
Save so encumbered. I wrote tales beside,
Carved many an article on cherry-stones
To suit light readers,—something in the lines
Revealing, it was said, the mallet-hand,
But that, I'll never vouch for. What you do
For bread, will taste of common grain, not grapes,
Although you have a vineyard in Champagne,—

prose; poetry; author; gender; profession of writing

JOHN RUSKIN (1819–1900)

LILIES OF QUEENS' GARDENS *(1864-5)*

Sesame and lilies

I want you to feel, with me, that whatever advantages we possess in the present day in the diffusion of education and of literature, can only be rightly used by any of us when we have apprehended clearly what education is to lead to, and literature to teach...

Believing that all literature and all education are only useful so far as they tend to confirm this calm, beneficent, and THEREFORE kingly, power--first, over ourselves, and, through ourselves, over all around us,--I am now going to ask you to consider with me farther, what special portion or kind of this royal authority, arising out of noble education, may rightly be possessed by women; and how far they also are called to a true queenly power,--not in their households merely, but over all within their sphere. And in what sense, if they rightly understood and exercised this royal or gracious influence, the order and beauty induced by such benignant power would justify us in speaking of the territories over which each of them reigned, as "Queens' Gardens"...

We cannot determine what the queenly power of women should be, until we are agreed what their ordinary power should be. We cannot consider how education may fit them for any widely extending duty, until we are agreed what is their true constant duty. And there never was a time when wilder words were spoken, or more vain imagination permitted, respecting this question--quite vital to all social happiness. The relations of the womanly to the manly nature, their different capacities of intellect or of virtue, seem never to have been yet estimated with entire consent. We hear of the "mission" and of the "rights" of Woman, as if these could ever be separate from the mission and the rights of Man--as if she and her lord were creatures of independent kind, and of irreconcilable claim. This, at least, is wrong. And not less wrong--perhaps even more foolishly wrong (for I will anticipate thus far what I hope to prove)--is the idea that woman is only the shadow and attendant image of her lord, owing him a thoughtless and servile obedience, and supported altogether in her weakness by the pre-eminence of his fortitude...

In all Christian ages which have been remarkable for their purity or progress, there has been absolute yielding of obedient devotion, by the lover, to his mistress. I say OBEDIENT;--not merely enthusiastic and worshipping in imagination, but entirely subject, receiving from the beloved woman, however young, not only the encouragement, the praise, and the reward of all toil, but, so far as any choice is open, or any question difficult of decision, the DIRECTION of all toil. That chivalry, to the abuse and dishonour of which are attributable primarily whatever is cruel in war, unjust in peace, or corrupt and ignoble in domestic relations; and to the original purity and power of which we owe the defence alike of faith, of law, and of love; that chivalry, I say, in its very first conception of honourable life, assumes the subjection of the young knight to the command-- should it even be the command in caprice--of his lady. It assumes this, because its masters knew that the first and necessary impulse of every truly taught and knightly heart is this of blind service to its lady: that where that true faith and captivity are not, all wayward and wicked passion must be; and that in this rapturous obedience to the single love of his youth, is the sanctification of all man's strength, and the continuance of all his purposes. And this, not because such obedience would be safe, or honourable, were it ever rendered to the unworthy; but because it ought to be impossible for every noble youth--it IS impossible for every one rightly trained--to love any one whose gentle counsel he cannot trust, or whose prayerful command he can hesitate to obey...

We are foolish, and without excuse foolish, in speaking of the 'superiority' of one sex to the other, as if they could be compared in similar things. Each has what the other has not: each completes the other, and is completed by the other: they are in nothing alike, and the happiness and perfection of both depends on each asking and receiving from the other what the other only can give.

Now their separate characters are briefly these. The man's power is active, progressive, defensive. He is eminently the doer, the creator, the discoverer, the defender. His intellect is for speculation and invention; his energy for adventure, for war, and for conquest, wherever war is just, wherever conquest necessary. But the woman's power is for rule, not for battle,-- and her intellect is not for invention or creation, but for sweet ordering, arrangement, and decision. She sees the qualities of things, their claims, and their places. Her great function is

Praise; she enters into no contest, but infallibly adjudges the crown of contest. By her office, and place, she is protected from all danger and temptation. The man, in his rough work in open world, must encounter all peril and trial;--to him, therefore, must be the failure, the offence, the inevitable error: often he must be wounded, or subdued; often misled; and ALWAYS hardened. But he guards the woman from all this; within his house, as ruled by her, unless she herself has sought it, need enter no danger, no temptation, no cause of error or offence. This is the true nature of home--it is the place of Peace; the shelter, not only from all injury, but from all terror, doubt, and division. In so far as it is not this, it is not home; so far as the anxieties of the outer life penetrate into it, and the inconsistently-minded, unknown, unloved, or hostile society of the outer world is allowed by either husband or wife to cross the threshold, it ceases to be home; it is then only a part of that outer world which you have roofed over, and lighted fire in...

And wherever a true wife comes, this home is always round her. The stars only may be over her head; the glowworm in the night-cold grass may be the only fire at her foot; but home is yet wherever she is; and for a noble woman it stretches far round her, better than ceiled with cedar, or painted with vermilion, shedding its quiet light far, for those who else were homeless...

(II.) I have been trying, thus far, to show you what should be the place, and what the power of woman. Now, secondly, we ask, What kind of education is to fit her for these?

And if you indeed think this a true conception of her office and dignity, it will not be difficult to trace the course of education which would fit her for the one, and raise her to the other. The first of our duties to her--no thoughtful persons now doubt this,--is to secure for her such physical training and exercise as may confirm her health, and perfect her beauty; the highest refinement of that beauty being unattainable without splendour of activity and of delicate strength. To perfect her beauty, I say, and increase its power; it cannot be too powerful, nor shed its sacred light too far: only remember that all physical freedom is vain to produce beauty without a corresponding freedom of heart...

All such knowledge should be given her as may enable her to understand, and even to aid, the work of men: and yet it should be given, not as knowledge,--not as if it were, or could be, for her an object to know; but only to feel, and to judge. It is of no moment, as a matter of pride or perfectness in herself, whether she knows many languages or one; but it is of the utmost, that she should be able to show kindness to a stranger, and to understand the sweetness of a stranger's tongue. It is of no moment to her own worth or dignity that she should be acquainted with this science or that; but it is of the highest that she should be trained in habits of accurate thought; that she should understand the meaning, the inevitableness, and the loveliness of natural laws; and follow at least some one path of scientific attainment, as far as to the threshold of that bitter Valley of Humiliation, into which only the wisest and bravest of men can descend, owning themselves for ever children, gathering pebbles on a boundless shore. It is of little consequence how many positions of cities she knows, or how many dates of events, or names of celebrated persons--it is not the object of education to turn the woman into a dictionary; but it is deeply necessary that she should be taught to enter with her whole personality into the history she reads; to picture the passages of it vitally in her own bright imagination; to apprehend, with her fine instincts, the pathetic circumstances and dramatic relations, which the historian too often only eclipses by his reasoning, and disconnects by his arrangement…

There IS one dangerous science for women--one which they must indeed beware how they profanely touch--that of theology. Strange, and miserably strange, that while they are modest enough to doubt their powers, and pause at the threshold of sciences where every step is demonstrable and sure, they will plunge headlong, and without one thought of incompetency, into that science in which the greatest men have trembled, and the wisest erred. Strange, that they will complacently and pridefully bind up whatever vice or folly there is in them, whatever arrogance, petulance, or blind incomprehensiveness, into one bitter bundle of consecrated myrrh. Strange, in creatures born to be Love visible, that where they can know least, they will condemn, first, and think to recommend themselves to their Master, by crawling up the steps of His judgment-throne to divide it with Him…

I believe, then, with this exception, that a girl's education should be nearly, in its course and material of study, the same as a boy's; but quite differently directed. A woman, in any rank of life, ought to know whatever her husband is likely to know, but to know it in a different way. His command of it should be foundational and progressive; hers, general and accomplished for daily and helpful use. Not but that it would often be wiser in men to learn things in a womanly sort of way, for present use, and to seek for the discipline and training of their mental powers in such branches of study as will be afterwards fittest for social service; but, speaking broadly, a man ought to know any language or science he learns, thoroughly--while a woman ought to know the same language, or science, only so far as may enable her to sympathise in her husband's pleasures, and in those of his best friends...

And indeed, if there were to be any difference between a girl's education and a boy's, I should say that of the two the girl should be earlier led, as her intellect ripens faster, into deep and serious subjects: and that her range of literature should be, not more, but less frivolous; calculated to add the qualities of patience and seriousness to her natural poignancy of thought and quickness of wit; and also to keep her in a lofty and pure element of thought. I enter not now into any question of choice of books; only let us be sure that her books are not heaped up in her lap as they fall out of the package of the circulating library, wet with the last and lightest spray of the fountain of folly.

Or even of the fountain of wit; for with respect to the sore temptation of novel reading, it is not the badness of a novel that we should dread, so much as its over-wrought interest. The weakest romance is not so stupefying as the lower forms of religious exciting literature, and the worst romance is not so corrupting as false history, false philosophy, or false political essays. But the best romance becomes dangerous, if, by its excitement, it renders the ordinary course of life uninteresting, and increases the morbid thirst for useless acquaintance with scenes in which we shall never be called upon to act...

Keep the modern magazine and novel out of your girl's way: turn her loose into the old library every wet day, and let her alone. She will find what is good for her; you cannot: for there is just this difference between the making of a girl's character and a boy's--you may chisel a boy into shape, as you would a rock, or hammer him into it, if he be of a better kind, as you would a piece of bronze. But you cannot hammer a girl into anything. She grows as a flower does,--she will wither without sun; she will decay in her sheath, as a narcissus will, if you do not give her air enough; she may fall, and defile her head in dust, if you leave her without help at some moments of her life; but you cannot fetter her; she must take her own fair form and way, if she take any, and in mind as in body...

Generally, we are under an impression that a man's duties are public, and a woman's private. But this is not altogether so. A man has a personal work or duty, relating to his own home, and a public work or duty, which is the expansion of the other, relating to the state. So a woman has a personal work or duty, relating to her own home, and a public work or duty, which is also the expansion of that...

The man's duty as a member of a commonwealth, is to assist in the maintenance, in the advance, in the defence of the state. The woman's duty, as a member of the commonwealth, is to assist in the ordering, in the comforting, and in the beautiful adornment of the state.

What the man is at his own gate, defending it, if need be, against insult and spoil, that also, not in a less, but in a more devoted measure, he is to be at the gate of his country, leaving his home, if need be, even to the spoiler, to do his more incumbent work there.

And, in like manner, what the woman is to be within her gates, as the centre of order, the balm of distress, and the mirror of beauty: that she is also to be without her gates, where order is more difficult, distress more imminent, loveliness more rare.

gender; reading; women and power; education; intellect; chivalry; rights; literature; morality; power; romantic; beauty; knowledge; theology; equality; public/private; education

MATTHEW ARNOLD
(1822–1888)

THE FUNCTION OF CRITICISM AT THE PRESENT TIME *(1864)*

…The critical power is of lower rank than the creative. True; but in assenting to this proposition, one or two things are to be kept in mind. It is undeniable that the exercise of a creative power, that a free creative activity, is the highest function of man; it is proved to be so by man's finding in it his true happiness. But it is undeniable, also, that men may have the sense of exercising this free creative activity in other ways than in producing great works of literature or art; if it were not so, all but a very few men would be shut out from the true happiness of all men. They may have it in well-doing, they may have it in learning, they may have it even in criticizing. This is one thing to be kept in mind. Another is, that the exercise of the creative power in the production of great works of literature or art, however high this exercise of it may rank, is not at all epochs and under all conditions possible; and that therefore labour may be vainly spent in attempting it, which might with more fruit be used in preparing for it, in rendering it possible. This creative power works with elements, with materials; what if it has not those materials, those elements, ready for its use? In that case it must surely wait till they are ready. Now, in literature,-- I will limit myself to literature, for it is about literature that the question arises,--the elements with which the creative power works are ideas; the best ideas on every matter which literature touches, current at the time. At any rate we may lay it down as certain that in modern literature no manifestation of the creative power not working with these can be very important or fruitful. And I say *current* at the time, not merely accessible at the time; for creative literary genius does not principally show itself in discovering new ideas: that is rather the business of the philosopher. The grand work of literary genius is a work of synthesis and exposition, not of analysis and discovery; its gift lies in the faculty of being happily inspired by a certain intellectual and spiritual atmosphere, by a certain order of ideas, when it finds itself in them; of dealing divinely with these ideas, presenting them in the most effective and attractive combinations,--making beautiful works with them, in short. But it must have the atmosphere, it must find itself amidst the order of ideas, in order to work freely; and these it is not so easy to command. This is why great creative epochs in literature are so rare, this is why there is so much that is unsatisfactory in the productions of many men of real genius; because, for the creation of a master-work of literature two powers must concur, the power of the man and the power of the moment, and the man is not enough without the moment; the creative power has, for its happy exercise, appointed elements, and those elements are not in its own control.

Nay, they are more within the control of the critical power. It is the business of the critical power, as I said in the words already quoted, "in all branches of knowledge, theology, philosophy, history, art, science, to see the object as in itself it really is". Thus it tends, at last, to make an intellectual situation of which the creative power can profitably avail itself. It tends to establish an order of ideas, if not absolutely true, yet true by comparison with that which it displaces; to make the best ideas prevail. Presently these new ideas reach society, the touch of truth is the touch of life, and there is a stir and growth everywhere; out of this stir and growth come the creative epochs of literature...

The Englishman has been called a political animal, and he values what is political and practical so much that ideas easily become objects of dislike in his eyes, and thinkers "miscreants", because ideas and thinkers have rashly meddled with politics and practice. This would be all very well if the dislike and neglect confined themselves to ideas transported out of their own sphere, and meddling rashly with practice; but they are inevitably extended to ideas as such, and to the whole life of intelligence; practice is everything, a free play of the mind is nothing. The notion of the free play of the mind upon all subjects being a pleasure in itself, being an object of desire, being an essential provider of elements without which a nation's spirit, whatever compensations it may have for them, must, in the long run, die of inanition, hardly enters into an Englishman's thoughts. It is noticeable that the word *curiosity*, which in other languages is used in a good sense, to mean, as a high and fine quality of man's nature, just this disinterested love of a free play of the mind on all subjects, for its own sake,--it is noticeable, I say, that this word has in our language no sense of the kind, no sense but a rather bad and disparaging one. But criticism, real criticism, is essentially the exercise of this very quality. It obeys an instinct prompting it to try to know the best that is known and thought in the world, irrespectively of practice, politics, and everything of the kind; and to value knowledge and thought as they approach this best, without the intrusion of any other considerations whatever.

critical; creative; literature; ideas; literary genius; beauty; tradition; poetry; politics; pleasure; the best that is known and thought in the world

ÉMILE ZOLA (1840–1902)

Preface to the second edition of 'Thérèse Raquin' (1868)
(translated by L. W. Tancock)

In *Therese Raquin* my aim has been to study temperaments and not characters. That is the whole point of the book. I have chosen people completely dominated by their nerves and blood, without free will, drawn into each action of their lives by the inexorable law of their physical nature...The sexual adventures of my hero and heroine are the satisfaction of a need, the murder they commit a consequence of their adultery, a consequence they accept just as wolves accept the slaughter of sheep. And finally, what I have had to call their remorse really amounts to a simple organic disorder, a revolt of the nervous system when strained to breaking-point. There is a complete absence of soul, I freely admit, since that is how I meant it to be.

I hope that by now it is becoming clear that my object has been first and foremost a scientific one...If the novel is read with care, it will be seen that each chapter is a study of a curious physiological case. In a word, I had only one desire: given a highly-sexed man and an unsatisfied woman, to uncover the animal side of them and see that alone, then throw them together in a violent drama and note down with scrupulous care the sensations and actions of these creatures. I simply applied to two living bodies the analytical method that surgeons apply to corpses.

You must allow that it is hard, on emerging from such a toil, still wholly given over to the serious satisfactions of the search for truth, to hear people accuse one of having had no other object than the painting of obscene pictures. I found myself in the same position as those painters who copy the nude without themselves being touched by the slightest sexual feeling, and are quite astonished when a critic declares that he is scandalised by the lifelike bodies in their work…

…The group of naturalist writers to which I have the honour of belonging has enough courage and energy to produce powerful works containing their own defence.

character; scientific method; truth; naturalism

MATTHEW ARNOLD
(1822–1888)

PREFACE TO CULTURE AND ANARCHY
(1869)

The whole scope of the essay is to recommend culture as the great help out of our present difficulties; culture being a pursuit of our total perfection by means of getting to know, on all the matters which most concern us, the best which has been thought and said in the world, and, through this knowledge, turning a stream of fresh and free thought upon our stock notions and habits, which we now follow staunchly but mechanically, vainly imagining that there is a virtue in following them staunchly which makes up for the mischief of following them mechanically. This, and this alone, is the scope of the following essay. I say again here, what I have said in the pages which follow, that from the faults and weaknesses of bookmen a notion of something bookish, pedantic, and futile has got itself more or less connected with the word culture, and that it is a pity we cannot use a word more perfectly free from all shadow of reproach. And yet, futile as are many bookmen, and helpless as books and reading often prove for bringing nearer to perfection those who use them, one must, I think, be struck more and more, the longer one lives, to find how much, in our present society, a man's life of each day depends for its solidity and value on whether he reads during that day, and, far more still, on what he reads during it. More and more he who examines himself will find the difference it makes to him, at the end of any given day, whether or no he has pursued his avocations throughout it without reading at all; and whether or no, having read something, he has read the newspapers only. This, however, is a matter for each man's private conscience and experience. If a man without books or reading, or reading nothing but his letters and the newspapers, gets nevertheless a fresh and free play of the best thoughts upon his stock notions and habits, he has got culture…

culture; perfection; value judgement; pedantry; reading; the best that has been thought and said in the world

… Culture is then properly described not as having its origin in curiosity, but as having its origin in the love of perfection; it is a study of perfection. It moves by the force, not merely or primarily of the scientific passion for pure knowledge, but also of the moral and social passion for doing good…

The pursuit of perfection, then, is the pursuit of sweetness and light. He who works for sweetness works in the end for light also; he who works for light works in the end for sweetness also. But he who works for sweetness and light united, works to make reason and the will of God prevail. He who works for machinery, he who works for hatred, works only for confusion. Culture looks beyond machinery, culture hates hatred; culture has but one great passion, the passion for sweetness and light. Yes, it has one yet greater!-- the passion for making them prevail. It is not satisfied till we all come to a perfect man; it knows that the sweetness and light of the few must be imperfect until the raw and unkindled masses of humanity are touched with sweetness and light. If I have not shrunk from saying that we must work for sweetness and light, so neither have I shrunk from saying that we must have a broad basis, must have sweetness and light for as many as possible. Again and again I have insisted how those are the happy moments of humanity, how those are the marking epochs of a people's life, how those are the flowering times for literature and art and all the creative power of genius, when there is a national glow of life and thought, when the whole of society is in the fullest measure permeated by thought, sensible to beauty, intelligent and alive. Only it must be real thought and real beauty; real sweetness and real light. Plenty of people will try to give the masses, as they call them, an intellectual food prepared and adapted in the way they think proper for the actual condition of the masses. The ordinary popular literature is an example of this way of working on the masses. Plenty of people will try to indoctrinate the masses with the set of ideas and judgments constituting the creed of their own profession or party. Our religious and political organisations give an example of this way of working on the masses. I condemn neither way; but culture works differently. It does not try to teach down to the level of inferior classes; it does not try to win them for this or that sect of its own, with ready-made judgments and watchwords. It seeks to do away with classes; to make all live in an atmosphere of sweetness and light, and use ideas, as it uses them itself, freely,--to be nourished and not bound by them.

This is the social idea; and the men of culture are the true apostles of equality. The great men of culture are those who have had a passion for diffusing, for making prevail, for carrying from one end of society to the other, the best knowledge, the best ideas of their time; who have laboured to divest knowledge of all that was harsh, uncouth, difficult, abstract, professional, exclusive; to humanise it, to make it efficient outside the clique of the cultivated and learned, yet still remaining the best knowledge and thought of the time, and a true source, therefore, of sweetness and light...

culture; curiosity; vanity; morality; ethics; perfection; sweetness and light; poetry; religion; popular literature; ideas; the masses; class

THE STUDY OF POETRY *(1880)*

…We should conceive of poetry worthily, and more highly than it has been the custom to conceive of it. We should conceive of it as capable of higher uses, and called to higher destinies than those which in general men have assigned to it hitherto. More and more mankind will discover that we have to turn to poetry to interpret life for us, to console us, to sustain us. Without poetry, our science will appear incomplete; and most of what now passes with us for religion and philosophy will be replaced by poetry. Science, I say, will appear incomplete without it…

For in poetry the distinction between excellent and inferior, sound and unsound or only half-sound, true and untrue or only half-true, is of paramount importance. It is of paramount importance because of the high destinies of poetry. In poetry, as a criticism of life under the conditions fixed for such a criticism by the laws of poetic truth and poetic beauty, the spirit of our race will find, we have said, as time goes on and as other helps fail, its consolation and stay. But the consolation and stay will be of power in proportion to the power of the criticism of life. And the criticism of life will be of power in proportion as the poetry conveying it is excellent rather than inferior, sound rather than unsound or half-sound, true rather than untrue or half-true…

Yes; constantly in reading poetry, a sense for the best, the really excellent, and of the strength and joy to be drawn from it, should be present in our minds and should govern our estimate of what we read. But this real estimate, the only true one, is liable to be superseded, if we are not watchful, by two other kinds of estimate, the historic estimate and the personal estimate, both of which are fallacious. A poet or a poem may count to us historically, they may count to us on grounds personal to ourselves, and they may count to us really. They may count to us historically. The course of development of a nation's language, thought, and poetry, is profoundly interesting; and by regarding a poet's work as a stage in this course of development we may easily bring ourselves to make it of more importance as poetry than in itself it really is, we may come to use a language of quite exaggerated praise in criticising it; in short, to over-rate it. So arises in our poetic judgments the fallacy caused by the estimate which we may call historic.

Then, again, a poet or a poem may count to us on grounds personal to ourselves. Our personal affinities, likings, and circumstances, have great power to sway our estimate of this or that poet's work, and to make us attach more importance to it as poetry than in itself it really possesses, because to us it is, or has been, of high importance. Here also we over-rate the object of our interest, and apply to it a language of praise which is quite exaggerated. And thus we get the source of a second fallacy in our poetic judgments--the fallacy caused by an estimate which we may call personal...

At any rate the end to which the method and the estimate are designed to lead, and from leading to which, if they do lead to it, they get their whole value,--the benefit of being able clearly to feel and deeply to enjoy the best, the truly classic, in poetry,--is an end, let me say it once more at parting, of supreme importance. We are often told that an era is opening in which we are to see multitudes of a common sort of readers, and masses of a common sort of literature; that such readers do not want and could not relish anything better than such literature, and that to provide it is becoming a vast and profitable industry. Even if good literature entirely lost currency with the world, it would still be abundantly worth while to continue to enjoy it by oneself. But it never will lose currency with the world, in spite of momentary appearances; it never will lose supremacy. Currency and supremacy are insured to it, not indeed by the world's deliberate and conscious choice, but by something far deeper,--by the instinct of self-preservation in humanity.

poetry as criticism of life; poetry; science; value judgement; historic estimate; personal estimate; fallacies; passion; common reader; truth

WILLIAM JAMES (1842–1910)

Talks to teachers on psychology; and to students on some of life's ideals (1892)

II. The stream of consciousness

...Now the *immediate* fact which psychology, the science of mind, has to study is also the most general fact. It is the fact that in each of us, when awake (and often when asleep), *some kind of consciousness is always going on.* There is a stream, a succession of states, or waves, or fields (or of whatever you please to call them), of knowledge, of feeling, of desire, of deliberation, etc., that constantly pass and repass, and that constitute our inner life. The existence of this stream is the primal fact, the nature and origin of it form the essential problem, of our science. So far as we class the states or fields of consciousness, write down their several natures, analyse their contents into elements, or trace their habits of succession, we are on the descriptive or analytic level. So far as we ask where they come from or why they are just what they are, we are on the explanatory level.

In these talks with you, I shall entirely neglect the questions that come up on the explanatory level. It must be frankly confessed that in no fundamental sense do we know where our successive fields of consciousness come from, or why they have the precise inner constitution which they do have. They certainly follow or accompany our brain states, and of course their special forms are determined by our past experiences and education. But, if we ask just *how* the brain conditions them, we have not the remotest inkling of an answer to give; and, if we ask just how the education moulds the brain, we can speak but in the most abstract, general, and conjectural terms. On the other hand, if we should say that they are due to a spiritual being called our Soul, which reacts on our brain states by these peculiar forms of spiritual energy, our words would be familiar enough, it is true; but I think you will agree that they would offer little genuine explanatory meaning. The truth is that we really *do not know* the answers to the problems on the explanatory level, even though in some directions of inquiry there may be promising speculations to be found. For our present purposes I shall therefore dismiss them entirely, and turn to mere description. This state of things was what I had in mind when, a moment ago, I said there was no 'new psychology' worthy of the name.

We have thus fields of consciousness,--that is the first general fact; and the second general fact is that the concrete fields are always complex. They contain sensations of our bodies and of the objects around us, memories of past experiences and thoughts of distant things, feelings of satisfaction and dissatisfaction, desires and aversions, and other emotional conditions, together with determinations of the will, in every variety of permutation and combination. In most of our concrete states of consciousness all these different classes of ingredients are found simultaneously present to some degree, though the relative proportion they bear to one another is very shifting. One state will seem to be composed of hardly anything but sensations, another of hardly anything but memories, etc. But around the sensation, if one consider carefully, there will always be some fringe of thought or will, and around the memory some margin or penumbra of emotion or sensation.

In most of our fields of consciousness there is a core of sensation that is very pronounced. You, for example, now, although you are also thinking and feeling, are getting through your eyes sensations of my face and figure, and through your ears sensations of my voice. The sensations are the *centre* or *focus*, the thoughts and feelings the *margin*, of your actually present conscious field.

On the other hand, some object of thought, some distant image, may have become the focus of your mental attention even while I am speaking,--your mind, in short, may have wandered from the lecture; and, in that case, the sensations of my face and voice, although not absolutely vanishing from your conscious field, may have taken up there a very faint and marginal place...

In the successive mutations of our fields of consciousness, the process by which one dissolves into another is often very gradual, and all sorts of inner rearrangements of contents occur. Sometimes the focus remains but little changed, while the margin alters rapidly. Sometimes the focus alters, and the margin stays. Sometimes focus and margin change places. Sometimes, again, abrupt alterations of the whole field occur. There can seldom be a sharp description. All we know is that, for the most part, each field has a sort of practical unity for its possessor, and that from this practical point of view we can class a field with other fields similar to it, by calling it a state of emotion, of perplexity, of sensation, of abstract thought, of volition, and the like.

Vague and hazy as such an account of our stream of consciousness may be, it is at least secure from positive error and free from admixture of conjecture or hypothesis. An influential school of psychology, seeking to avoid haziness of outline, has tried to make things appear more exact and scientific by making the analysis more sharp.

psychology; consciousness; stream of consciousness; soul; fields of consciousness; senses; sensation; theory of ideas; focus

WALTER BESANT (1836–1901)

THE ART OF FICTION *(1884)*

…Let us, however, go outside this room, among the multitudes by whom a novelist has never been considered an artist at all. To them the claim that a great novelist should be considered to occupy the same level as a great musician, a great painter, or a great poet, would appear at first a thing ludicrous and even painful. Consider for a moment how the world at large regards the novelist.

He is, in their eyes, a person who tells stories, just as they used to regard the actor as a man who tumbled on the stage to make the audience laugh, and a musician as a man who fiddled to make the people dance. It is therefore quite easy to understand why the art of novel-writing has always been, by the general mass, undervalued…no one ever hears of honors being bestowed upon novelists. Neither Thackeray nor Dickens was ever, so far as I know, offered a Peerage…Then again, in the modern craze which exists for every kind of art…amateur novelists alone regard their Art as one which is learned by intuition…novelists are not associated as are painters…they have no President or Academy; and they do not themselves seem desirous of being treated as followers of a special Art…

It is, I acknowledge, a kindly contempt – even an affectionate contempt; it is the contempt which the practical man feels for the dreamer, the strong man for the weak, the man who can do for the man who can only look on and talk.

The general – the Philistine – view of the Profession is, first of all, that it is not one which a scholar and a man of serious views should take up: the telling of stories is inconsistent with a well-balanced mind…the intellect of a novelist, it is felt, if he have any intellect at all, which is doubtful, must be one of the most frivolous and lightest kind…How can that be an Art, they might ask, which has no lecturers or teachers, no school or college or Academy, no recognised rules, no text-books, and is not taught in any University?

…The modern novel converts abstract ideas into living models; it gives ideas, it strengthens faith, it preaches a higher morality than is seen in the actual world; it commands the emotions of pity, admiration, and terror; it creates and keeps alive the sense of sympathy; it is the universal teacher; it is the only book which the great mass of reading mankind ever do read; it is the only way in which people can learn what other men and women are like; it redeems their lives from dullness, puts thoughts, desires, knowledge, and even ambitions into their ears: it teaches them to talk, and enriches their speech with epigrams, anecdotes and illustrations…

As for the field with which this Art of Fiction occupies itself, it is, if you please, nothing less than the whole of Humanity. The novelist studies men and women; he is concerned with their actions and their thoughts, their errors and their follies, their greatness and their meanness; the countless forms of beauty and constantly varying moods to be seen among them; the forces which act upon them; the passions, prejudices, hopes and fears which pull them this way and that…The very first rule in Fiction is that the human interest must absolutely absorb everything else…

We come next to speak of the Laws which govern this art… which must necessarily be acquired by every writer of Fiction before he can even hope for success…

First, and before everything else, there is the Rule that everything in Fiction which is invented and is not the result of personal experience and observation is worthless…in modern Fiction, whose sole end, aim, and purpose is to portray humanity and human character, the design must be in accordance with the customs and general practice of living men and women under any proposed set of circumstances and conditions. That is to say, the characters must be real, and such as might be met with in actual life, or at least, the natural developments of such people as any of us might meet; their actions must be natural and consistent; the conditions of place, of manners, and of thought must be drawn from personal observation…This is a very simple Rule, but one to which there should be no exception – never to go beyond your own experience. Remember that most of the people who read novels, and know nothing about the art of writing them, recognise before any other quality that of fidelity: the greatness of a novelist they measure chiefly by the knowledge of the world displayed in his pages; the highest praise they can bestow upon him is that he has drawn the story to the life…

This being so, the first thing which has to be acquired is the art of description. It seems easy to describe; any one, it seems, can set down what he sees. But consider. How much does he see?…The unpractised eye sees nothing, or next to nothing… we must not only observe, but we must select…

Fidelity, therefore, can only be assured by acquiring the art of observation, which further assists in filling the mind with stored experience…

What is next required is the power of Selection. Can this be taught? I think not, at least I do not know how, unless it is by reading. In every Art, selection requires that kind of special fitness for the Art which is included in the much abused word Genius. In Fiction the power of selection required a large share of the dramatic sense. Those who already possess this faculty will not go wrong if they bear in mind the simple rule that nothing should be admitted which does not advance the story, illustrate the characters, bring into stronger relief the hidden forces which act upon them, their emotions, their passions, and their intentions…

Closely connected with selection is dramatic presentation. Given a situation, it should be the first care of the writer to present it as dramatically, that is to say as forcibly, as possible. The grouping and setting of the picture, the due subordination of description to dialogue, the rapidity of the action, those things which naturally suggest themselves to the practised eye, deserve to be very carefully considered by the beginner. It fact, a novel is like a play: it may be divided into scenes and acts, tableaus and situations, separated by the end of the chapter, instead of the drop-scene: the writer is the dramatist, stage-manager, scene-painter, actor, and carpenter, all in one…

The next simple Rule is that the drawing of each figure must be clear in outline, and, even if only sketched, must be sketched without hesitation. This can only be done when the writer himself sees his figures clearly. Characters in fiction do not, it must be understood, spring Minerva-like from the brain. They grow; they grow sometimes slowly, sometimes quickly…

how possible, how capable of development, how real becomes a true figure, truly understood by the creator, and truly depicted! Do we not know what they would say and think under all conceivable conditions? We can dress them as we will; we can place them in any circumstances of life; we can always trust them because they will never fail us, never disappoint us, never change, because we understand them so thoroughly. So well do we know them that they become our advisors, our guides, and our best friends, on whom we model ourselves, our thoughts, and our actions…

To sum up these few preliminary and general laws. The Art of Fiction requires first of all the power of description, truth, and fidelity, observation, selection, clearness of conception, and of outline, dramatic grouping, directness of purpose, a profound belief on the part of the story-teller in the reality of his story, and beauty of workmanship. It is, moreover, an Art which requires of those who follow it seriously that they must be unceasingly occupied in studying the ways of mankind, the social laws, the religions, philosophies, tendencies, thoughts, prejudices, superstitions of men and women. They must consider as many of the forces which act upon classes and upon individuals as they can discover; they should be always trying to put themselves into the place of another; they must be as inquisitive and as watchful as a detective, as suspicious as a criminal lawyer, as eager for knowledge as a physicist, and withal fully possessed of that spirit to which nothing appears mean, nothing contemptible, nothing unworthy of study, which belongs to human nature.

…I am certain that if these laws were better known and more generally studied, a very large proportion of the bad works of which our critics complain would not be produced at all. And I am in great hopes that one effect of the establishment of the newly founded Society of Authors will be to keep young writers of fiction from rushing too hastily into print, to help them in the right understanding of their Art and its principles, and to guide them into true practice of their principles while they are still young, their imaginations strong, and their personal experiences as yet not wasted in foolish failures…

morality; poetry; novelist; story; the novel; intuition; personal experience; characters; reality; imitation; write what you know; description; selection; dialogue; action; observation; sympathy; truth; human interest

HENRY JAMES (1843–1916)

THE ART OF FICTION *(1900)*

…Only a short time ago it might have been supposed that the English novel was not what the French call *discutable*. It had no air of having a theory, a conviction, a consciousness of itself behind it – of being the expression of an artistic faith, the result of choice and comparison…But within a year or two, for some reason or other, there have been signs of returning animation – the era of discussion would appear to have been to a certain extent opened. Art lives upon discussion, upon experiment, upon curiosity, upon variety of attempt, upon the exchange of views and the comparison of standpoints…The successful application of any art is a delightful spectacle, but the theory, too, is interesting; and though there is a great deal of the latter without the former, I suspect that there has never been a genuine success that has not had a latent core of conviction…Mr Besant has set an excellent example in saying what he thinks, for his part, about the way fiction should be written…

It is still expected, though perhaps people are ashamed to say it, that a production which is after all only a 'make believe' (for what else is a 'story'?) shall be in some degree apologetic – shall renounce the pretension of attempting really to compete with life…The only reason for the existence of a novel is that it *does* compete with life. When it ceases to compete as the canvas of a painter competes, it will have arrived at a very strange pass. It is not expected of the picture that it will make itself humble in order to be forgiven; and the analogy between the art of the painter and the art of the novelist is, so far as I am able to see, complete. Their inspiration is the same, their process (allowing for the different quality of the vehicle) is the same, their success is the same…as the picture is reality, so the novel is history… But history is also allowed to compete with life, as I say; it is not, any more than painting, expected to apologise. The subject-matter of fiction is stored up likewise in documents and records, and if it will not give itself away, as they say in California, I must speak with assurance, with the tone of the historian… to represent and illustrate the past, the actions of men, is the task of either writer, and the only difference that I can see is, in proportion as he succeeds, to the honor of the novelist, consisting as it does in his having more difficulty in collecting his evidence, which is so far from being purely literary. It seems to me to give him a great character, the fact that he has at once so much in common with the philosopher and the painter; this double analogy is a magnificent heritage…

…'Art', in our Protestant communities, where so many things have got so strangely twisted about, is supposed, in certain circles, to have some vaguely injurious effect upon those who make it an important consideration, who let it weigh in the balance. It is assumed to be opposed in some mysterious manner to morality, to amusement, to instruction…Literature should be either instructive or amusing, and there is in many minds an impression that these artistic pre-occupations, the search for form, contribute to neither end, interfere, indeed, with both. They are too frivolous to be edifying, and too serious to be diverting…

As I shall take the liberty of making but a single criticism of Mr Besant, whose tone is so full of the love of his art, I may as well have done with it at once. He seems to me to mistake in attempting to say so definitely beforehand what sort of an affair the good novel will be. To indicate the danger of such an error as that has been the purpose of these few pages; to suggest that certain traditions on the subject, applied *a priori*, have already had much to answer for, and that the good health of an art which undertakes so immediately to reproduce life must demand that it be perfectly free. It lives upon exercise, and the very meaning of exercise is freedom. The only obligation to which in advance we may hold a novel without incurring the accusation of being arbitrary, is that it be interesting. That general responsibility rests upon it, but it is the only one I can think of. The ways in which it is at liberty to accomplish this result (of interesting us) strike me as innumerable and such as can only suffer from being marked out, or fenced in, by prescription…A novel is in its broadest definition a personal impression of life; that, to begin with, constitutes its value, which is greater or less according to the intensity of the impression…The execution belongs to the author alone; it is what is most personal to him, and we measure him by that… His manner is his secret, not necessarily a deliberate one. He cannot disclose it, as a general thing, if he would; he would be at a loss to teach it to others. I say this with a due recollection of having insisted on the community of method of the artist who paints a picture and the artist who writes a novel. The painter *is* able to teach the rudiments of his practice, and it is possible, from the study of good work (granted the aptitude), both to learn how to paint and to learn how to write. Yet it remains true, without injury to the *rapprochement*, that the literary artist would be obliged to say to his pupil much more than the other, 'Ah, well, you must do it as you can!' It is a matter of degree, a matter of delicacy.

...The characters, the situation, which strike one as real, will be those that touch and interest one most, but the measure of reality is very difficult to fix...It goes without saying that you will not write a good novel unless you possess the sense of reality; but it will be difficult to give you a recipe for calling that sense into being. Humanity is immense, and reality has a myriad forms; the most one can affirm is that some of the flowers of fiction have the odor of it, and others have not...It is equally excellent and inconclusive to say that one must write from experience; to our suppositious aspirant such a declaration might savor of mockery. What kind of experience is intended, and where does it begin and end? Experience is never limited, and it is never complete; it is an immense sensibility, a kind of huge spider-web, of the finest silken threads, suspended in the chamber of consciousness and catching every air-borne particle in its tissue. It is the very atmosphere of the mind; and when the mind is imaginative – much more when it happens to be that of a man of genius – it takes to itself the faintest hints of life, it converts the very pulses of the air into revelations...The power to guess the unseen from the seen, to trace the implication of things, to judge the whole piece by the pattern, the condition of feeling life, in general, so completely that you are well on your way to knowing any particular corner of it – this cluster of gifts may almost be said to constitute experience, and they occur in country and in town, and in the most differing stages of education. If experience consists of impressions, it may be said that impressions *are* experience, just as (have we not seen it?) they are the very air we breathe...

One can speak from one's own taste, and I may therefore venture to say that the air of reality (solidity of specification) seems to me to be the supreme virtue of a novel– the merit in which all its other merits (including that conscious moral purpose of which Mr Besant speaks) helplessly and submissively depend. If it be not there, they are all as nothing, and if these be there they owe their effect to the success with which the author has produced the illusion of life. The cultivation of this success, the study of this exquisite process, form, to my taste, the beginning and the end of the art of the novelist. They are his inspiration, his despair, his reward, his torment, his delight. It is here, in very truth, that he competes with life; it is here that he competed with his brother, the painter, in *his* attempt to render the look of things, the look that conveys their meanings, to catch the color, the relief, the expression, the surface, the substance of the human spectacle...to 'render' the simplest surface, to produce the most momentary illusion, is a very complicated business...I cannot imagine composition existing in a series of blocks, nor conceive, in any novel worth discussing at all, a passage of description that is not in its intention narrative, a passage of dialogue that is not in its intention descriptive, a touch of truth of any sort that does not partake of the nature of incident, and an incident that derives its interest from any other source than the general and only source of the success of a work of art, – that of being illustrative. A novel is a living thing, all one and continuous, like every other organism, and in proportion as it lives it will be found, I think, that in each of the parts there is something of each of the other parts...There is an old-fashioned distinction between the novel of character and the novel of incident, which must have cost many a smile to the intending romancer who was keen about his work. It appears to me as little to the point as the equally celebrated distinction between the novel and the romance – to answer as little to any reality. There are bad novels and good novels, as there are bad pictures and good pictures; but that is the only distinction in which I see any meaning, and I can as little imagine speaking of a novel of character as I can imagine speaking of a picture of character. When one says picture, one says of character; when one says novel, one says of incident, and the terms may be transposed. What is character but the determination of incident? What is incident but the illustration of character?…It sounds almost puerile to say that some incidents are intrinsically much more important than others, and I need not take this precaution, after having professed my sympathy for the major ones, in remarking that the only classification of the novel that can be understood is the interesting and the uninteresting.

…The novel and the romance, the novel of incident and that of character – these separations appear to me to have been made by critics and readers for their own convenience, and to help them out of some of their difficulties, but to have little reality or interest for the producer, from whose point of view it is, of course, that we are attempting to consider the art of fiction…

Nothing, of course, will ever take the place of the good old fashion of 'liking' a work of art or not liking it; the more improved criticism will not abolish that primitive, that ultimate, test…I am quite at a loss to imagine anything (at any rate in this matter of fiction) that people *ought* to like or to dislike. Selection will be sure to take care of itself, for it has a constant motive behind it. That motive is simply experience. As people feel life, so they will feel the art that is most closely related to it. This closeness of relation is what we should never forget in talking of the effort of the novel. Many people speak of it as a factitious, artificial form, a product of ingenuity, the business of which is to alter and arrange the things that surround us, to translate them into conventional, traditional moulds. This, however, is a view of the matter which carries us but a very short way, condemns the art to an eternal repetition of a few familiar *clichés,* cuts short its development and leads us straight up to a dead wall. Catching the very note and trick, the strange irregular rhythms of life, that is the attempt whose strenuous force keeps Fiction upon her feet. In proportion as in what she offers us, we see life *without* rearrangement, do we feel that we are touching the truth; in proportion as we see it *with* arrangement do we feel that we are being put off with a substitute, a compromise and convention…Art is essentially selection, but it is a selection whose main care is to be typical, to be inclusive. For many people art means rose-colored windows, and selection means picking a bouquet for Mrs Grundy. They will tell you glibly that artistic considerations have nothing to do with the disagreeable, with the ugly; they will rattle off shallow commonplaces about the province of art and the limits of art, till you are moved to some wonder in return as to the province and the limits of ignorance. It appears to me that no one can ever have made a seriously artistic attempt without becoming conscious of an immense increase – a kind of revelation – of freedom. One perceives, in that case – by the light of a heavenly ray – that the province of art is all life, all feeling, all observation, all vision…

I cannot see what is meant by talking as if there were a part of a novel which is the story and part of it which for mystical reasons is not…This sense of the story being the idea, the starting-point of the novel, is the only one that I see in which it can be spoken of as something different from its organic whole; and since, in proportion as the work is successful, the idea permeates and penetrates it, informs and animates it, so that every word and every punctuation-point contribute directly to the expression, in that proportion do we lose our sense of the story being a blade which may be drawn more or less out of its sheath. The story and the novel, the idea and the form, are the needle and thread, and I never heard of a guild of tailors who recommended the use of the thread without the needle or the needle without the thread…

Like Mr Besant, I have left the question of the morality of the novel till the last, and at the last I find I have used up my space. It is a question surrounded with difficulties, as witness the very first that meets us, in the form of a definite question on the threshold. Vagueness, in such a discussion, is fatal, and what is the meaning of our morality and your conscious moral purpose? Will you not define your terms and explain how (a novel being a picture) a picture can be either moral or immoral?…We are discussing the Art of Fiction; questions of art are questions (in the widest sense) of execution; questions of morality are quite another affair, and will you not let us see how it is that you find it so easy to mix them up?…I may add that, in so far as Mr Besant perceives that in point of fact English Fiction has addressed itself preponderantly to these delicate questions, he will appear to many people to have made a vain discovery… In the English novel (by which I mean the American as well), more than in any other, there is a traditional difference between that which people know and that which they agree to admit they know, that which they see and that which they speak of, that which they feel to be a part of life and that which they allow to enter into literature…The essence of moral energy is to survey the whole field…

There is one point at which the moral sense and the artistic sense lie very near together; that is, in the light of the very obvious truth that the deepest quality of a work of art will always be the quality of the mind of the producer. In proportion as that mind is rich and noble, will the novel, the picture, the statue, partake of the substance of beauty and truth. To be constituted of such elements is, to my vision, to have purpose enough. No good novel will ever proceed from a superficial mind; that seems to me an axiom which, for the artist in fiction, will cover all needful moral ground…

novel; story; life; reality; history; subject matter; art; morality; teaching; characters; situation; experience; consciousness; subtexts; meaning; description; narrative; incident; value judgement; criticism; selection; the typical; truth; moral sensibility

PART FIVE

Twentieth Century

A. C. BRADLEY (1851–1935)

Poetry for Poetry's sake *(1901)*

What then does the formula 'Poetry for poetry's sake' tell us
about this experience? It says, as I understand it, these things.
First, this experience is an end in itself, is worth having on its
own account, has an intrinsic value. Next, its *poetic* value is this
intrinsic worth alone. Poetry may also have an ulterior value as
a means to culture or religion; because it conveys instruction, or
softens the passions, or furthers a good cause; because it brings
the poet fame or money or a quiet conscience. So much the
better; let it be valued for those reasons too. But its ulterior
worth neither is nor can directly determine its poetic worth
as a satisfying imaginative experience; and this is to be judged
entirely from within. And to these two positions the formula
would add, though not of necessity, a third. The consideration
of ulterior ends whether by the poet in the act of composing or
by the reader in the act of experiencing, ends to lower poetic
value. It does so because it tends to change the nature of poetry
by taking it out of its own atmosphere. For its nature is to be
not a part, nor yet a copy of the real world (as we commonly
understand that phrase) but to be a world by itself, independent,
complete autonomous; and to possess it fully you must enter

that world, conform to its laws, and ignore for the time the beliefs, aims, and particular conditions which belong to you in the other world of reality.

...our formula may be accused of cutting poetry away from its connection with life. And this accusation raises so huge a problem that I must ask leave to be dogmatic as well as brief. There is plenty of connection between life and poetry, but it is, so to say, a connection underground. The two may be called different forms of the same thing: one of them having (in the usual sense) reality, but seldom fully satisfying imagination; while the other offers something which satisfies imagination but has not full 'reality'. They are parallel developments which nowhere meet, or, if I may use loosely a word which will be serviceable later, they are analogues. Hence we understand one by help of the other; but hence also, poetry neither is life, nor, strictly speaking, a copy of it. They differ not only because one has more mass and the other a more perfect shape, but because they have different *kinds* of existence. The one touches us as beings occupying a given position in space and time, and having feelings, desires, and purposes due to that position: it appeals to imagination, but appeals to much besides. What meets us in poetry has not a position in the same series of time and space, or, if it has or had such a position, it is taken apart from much that belonged to it there; and therefore it makes no direct appeal to those feelings, desires, and purposes, but speaks only to contemplative imagination – imagination the reverse of empty or emotionless, imagination saturated with the result of 'real' experience, but still contemplative. This, no doubt, one main reason why poetry has poetic value for us is that it presents to us in its own way something which we meet in another form in nature or life; and yet the test of its poetic value for us lies simply in the question whether it satisfies our imagination; the rest of us, our knowledge of conscience, for example, judging it only so far as they appear transmuted in our imagination.

mimesis; art; life; poetry; contemplation; imagination; ideology; social structure; difference; specialisation

HENRY JAMES (1843–1916)

PREFACE TO THE PORTRAIT OF A LADY
(1908)

...There is, I think, no more nutritive or suggestive truth in this connexion than that of the perfect dependence of the "moral" sense of a work of art on the amount of felt life concerned in producing it. The question comes back thus, obviously, to the kind and the degree of the artist's prime sensibility, which is the soil out of which his subject springs. The quality and capacity of that soil, its ability to "grow" with due freshness and straightness any vision of life, represents, strongly or weakly, the projected morality. That element is but another name for the more or less close connexion of the subject with some mark made on the intelligence, with some sincere experience. By which, at the same time, of course, one is far from contending that this enveloping air of the artist's humanity—which gives the last touch to the worth of the work--is not a widely and wondrously varying element; being on one occasion a rich and magnificent medium and on another a comparatively poor and ungenerous one. Here we get exactly the high price of the novel as a literary form--its power not only, while preserving that form with closeness, to range through all the differences of the individual relation to its general subject-matter, all the varieties of outlook on life, of disposition to reflect and project, created by conditions that are never the same from man to man (or, so far as that goes, from man to woman), but positively to appear more true to its character in proportion as it strains, or tends to burst, with a latent extravagance, its mould.

The house of fiction has in short not one window, but a million—a number of possible windows not to be reckoned, rather; every one of which has been pierced, or is still pierceable, in its vast front, by the need of the individual vision and by the pressure of the individual will. These apertures, of dissimilar shape and size, hang so, all together, over the human scene that we might have expected of them a greater sameness of report than we find. They are but windows at the best, mere holes in a dead wall, disconnected, perched aloft; they are not hinged doors opening straight upon life. But they have this mark of their own that at each of them stands a figure with a pair of eyes, or at least with a field-glass, which forms, again and again, for observation, a unique instrument, insuring to the person making use of it an impression distinct from every other. He and his neighbours are watching the same show, but one seeing more where the other sees less, one seeing black where the other sees white, one seeing big where the other sees small, one seeing coarse where the other sees fine. And so on, and so on; there is fortunately no saying on what, for the particular pair of eyes, the window may NOT open; "fortunately" by reason, precisely, of this incalculability of range. The spreading field, the human scene, is the "choice of subject"; the pierced aperture, either broad or balconied or slit-like and low-browed, is the "literary form"; but they are, singly or together, as nothing without the posted presence of the watcher--without, in other words, the consciousness of the artist. Tell me what the artist is, and I will tell you of what he has BEEN conscious. Thereby I shall express to you at once his boundless freedom and his "moral" reference.

morality; felt life; sensibility; intelligence; humanity; novel; house of fiction; metaphor; point of view; consciousness; perspective

SIR ARTHUR QUILLER-COUCH (1863–1944)

ON THE ART OF WRITING *(1916)*

Preface

…Literature is not a mere Science, to be studied; but an Art, to be practised…

Inaugural

…Let me, then, lay down two or three principles by which I propose to be guided. (1) For the first principle of all I put to you that in studying any work of genius we should begin by taking it *absolutely*; that is to say, with minds intent on discovering just what the author's mind intended…

My next two principles may be more briefly stated. (2) I propose next, then, that since our investigations will deal largely with style, that curiously personal thing; and since (as I have said) they cannot in their nature be readily brought to rule-of-thumb tests, and may therefore so easily be suspected of evading all tests, of being mere dilettantism; I propose (I say) that my pupils and I rebuke this suspicion by constantly aiming at the concrete, at the study of such definite beauties as we can see presented in print under our eyes; always seeking the author's intention, but eschewing, for the present at any rate, all general definitions and theories, through the sieve of which the particular achievement of genius is so apt to slip. And having excluded them at first in prudence, I make little doubt we shall go on to exclude them in pride. Definitions, formulæ (some would add, creeds) have their use in any society in that they restrain the ordinary unintellectual man from making himself a public nuisance with his private opinions. But they go a very little way in helping the man who has a real sense of prose or verse…

As Literature is an Art and therefore not to be pondered only, but practised, so ours is a living language and therefore to be kept alive, supple, active in all honourable use. The orator can yet sway men, the poet ravish them, the dramatist fill their lungs with salutary laughter or purge their emotions by pity or terror. The historian 'superinduces upon events the charm of order'. The novelist--well, even the novelist has his uses; and I would warn you against despising any form of art which is alive and pliant in the hands of men…Of the Novel, at any rate--whether we like it or not--we have to admit that it does hold a commanding position in the literature of our times…

literature; science; art; principles; writing; authorial intention; style; theory; genius; language; novel

Lecture 11 The practice of writing.

…Well, then, I propose to you that, English Literature being (as we agreed) an Art, with a living and therefore improvable language for its medium or vehicle, a part--and no small part--of our business is *to practise it.* Yes, I seriously propose to you that here in Cambridge we *practise writing*: that we practise it not only for our own improvement, but to make, or at least try to make, appropriate, perspicuous, accurate, persuasive writing a recognisable hall-mark of anything turned out by our English School. By all means let us study the great writers of the past for their own sakes; but let us study them for our guidance; that we, in our turn, having (it is to be hoped) something to say in our span of time, say it worthily, not dwindling out the large utterance of Shakespeare or of Burke.

Now I started by proposing that we try together to make appropriate, perspicuous, accurate, persuasive writing a hall-mark of anything turned out by our English School here, and I would add (growing somewhat hardier) a hall-mark of all Cambridge style so far as our English School can influence it. I chose these four epithets *accurate, perspicuous, persuasive, appropriate*, with some care, of course as my duty was; and will assume that by this time we are agreed to desire *appropriateness*. Now for the other three:--

Perspicuity. I shall waste no words on the need of this: since the first aim of speech is to be understood. The more clearly you write the more easily and surely you will be understood. I propose to demonstrate to you further, in a minute or so, that the more clearly you write the more clearly you will understand yourself. But a sufficient reason has been given in ten words why you should desire perspicuity.

Accuracy. Did I not remind myself in my first lecture, that Cambridge is the home of accurate scholarship? Surely no Cambridge man would willingly be a sloven in speech, oral or written? Surely here, if anywhere, should be acknowledged of all what Newman says of the classics, that 'a certain unaffected neatness and propriety and grace of diction may be required of any author, for the same reason that a certain attention to dress is expected of every gentleman.' After all, what are the chief differentiae between man and the brute creation but that he clothes himself, that he cooks his food, that he uses articulate speech? Let us cherish and improve all these distinctions.

... let me remind you that you cannot use the briefest, the humblest process of thought, cannot so much as resolve to take your bath hot or cold, or decide what to order for breakfast, without forecasting it to yourself in some form of words. Words are, in fine, the only currency in which we can exchange thought even with ourselves. Does it not follow, then, that the more accurately we use words the closer definition we shall give to our thoughts? Does it not follow that by drilling ourselves to write perspicuously we train our minds to clarify their thought? Does it not follow that some practice in the deft use of words, with its correspondent defining of thought, may well be ancillary even to the study of Natural Science in a University?

But I have another word for our men of science. It was inevitable, perhaps, that Latin--so long the Universal Language--should cease in time to be that in which scientific works were written. It was impossible, perhaps, to substitute, by consent, some equally neat and austere modern language, such as French. But when it became an accepted custom for each nation to use its own language in scientific treatises, it certainly was not foreseen that men of science would soon be making discoveries at a rate which left their skill in words outstripped; that having to invent their terms as they went along, yet being careless and contemptuous of a science in which they have no training, they would bombast out our dictionaries with monstrously invented words that not only would have made Quintilian stare and gasp, but would affront the recently literate of any age...

Let me revert to our list of the qualities necessary to good writing, and come to the last--*Persuasiveness;* of which you may say, indeed, that it embraces the whole--not only the qualities of propriety, perspicuity, accuracy, we have been considering, but many another, such as harmony, order, sublimity, beauty of diction; all in short that--writing being an art, not a science, and therefore so personal a thing--may be summed up under the word *Charm.* Who, at any rate, does not seek after Persuasion? It is the aim of all the arts and, I suppose, of all exposition of the sciences; nay, of all useful exchange of converse in our daily life.

In asking you to practise the written word, I began with such low but necessary things as propriety, perspicuity, accuracy. But *persuasion*--the highest form of persuasion at any rate-- cannot be achieved without a sense of beauty. And now I shoot a second rapid--.... *I want you to practise verse, and to practise it assiduously.* I am quite serious...

writing instruction; literary study; perspicuity; clarity; accuracy; scholarship; language; science; persuasiveness; charm; genius; art versus science

Lecture V
Interlude: on jargon

...to write Jargon is to be perpetually shuffling around in the fog and cotton-wool of abstract terms...to beat the air because it is easier than to flesh your sword in the thing. The first virtue, the touchstone of a masculine style, is its use of the active verb and the concrete noun. When you write in the active voice, 'They gave him a silver teapot,' you write as a man. When you write 'He was made the recipient of a silver teapot,' you write jargon. But at the beginning set even higher store on the concrete noun...

A lesson about writing your language may go deeper than language; for language (as in a former lecture I tried to preach to you) is your reason...So long as you prefer abstract words, which express other men's summarised concepts of things, to concrete ones which as near as can be reached to things themselves and are the first-hand material for your thoughts, you will remain, at the best, writers at second-hand. If your language be Jargon, your intellect, if not your whole character, will almost certainly correspond. Where your mind should go straight, it will dodge: the difficulties it should approach with a fair front and grip with a firm hand it will be seeking to evade or circumvent. For the Style is the Man, and where a man's treasure is there his heart, and his brain, and his writing, will be also.

jargon; abstractions; language; intellect; gender; masculine style; active verbs

Lecture VII, Some principles reaffirmed

We laid down certain rules to help us in the way of straight Prose:

(1) *Always always prefer the concrete word to the abstract.*
(2) *Almost always prefer the direct word to the circumlocution.*

(3) *Generally, use transitive verbs, that strike their object; and use them in the active voice, eschewing the stationary passive, with its little auxiliary its's and was's, and its participles getting into the light of your adjectives, which should be few. For, as a rough law, by his use of the straight verb and by his economy of adjectives you can tell a man's style, if it be masculine or neuter, writing or 'composition'.*

The authors of that capital handbook "The King's English," which I have already recommended to you, add two rules:--

(4) *Prefer the short word to the long.*
(5) *Prefer the Saxon word to the Romance.*

...Now by attending to the few plain rules given above you may train yourselves to write sound, straightforward, work-a-day English. But if you would write melodious English, I fear the gods will require of you what they ought to have given you at birth--something of an ear. Yet the most of us have ears, of sorts; and I believe that, though we can only acquire it by assiduous practice, the most of us can wonderfully improve our talent of the ear.

rules; prose; concrete; abstract; precepts; writing

VIRGINIA WOOLF (1882–1941)

A ROOM OF ONE'S OWN *(1928)*

But, you may say, we asked you to speak about women and fiction – what has that got to do with a room of one's own? I will try to explain. When you asked me to speak about women and fiction I sat down on the banks of a river and began to wonder what the words meant. They might mean simply a few remarks about Fanny Burney; a few more about Jane Austen; a tribute to the Brontes and a sketch of Haworth Parsonage under snow; some witticisms if possible about Miss Mitford; a respectful allusion to George Eliot; a reference to Mrs Gaskell and one would have done. But at second sight the words seemed not so simple. The title women and fiction might mean, and you may have meant it to mean, women and what they are like; or it might mean women and the fiction they write; or it might mean women and the fiction that is written about them; or it might mean that somehow all three are inextricably mixed together and you want me to consider them in that light. But when I began to consider the subject in this last way, which seemed the most interesting, I soon saw that it had one fatal drawback. I should never be able to fulfil what is, I understand, the first duty of a lecturer – to hand you after an hour's discourse a nugget of pure truth to wrap up between the pages of your notebooks and keep on the mantelpiece for ever. All I could do was to offer you an opinion upon one minor point – a woman must have money and a room of her own if she is to write fiction; and that, as you will see, leaves the great problem of the true nature of woman and the true nature of fiction unresolved. I have shirked the duty of coming to a conclusion upon these two questions – women and fiction remain, so far as I am concerned, unsolved problems…

…I could not help thinking, as I looked at the works of Shakespeare on the shelf, that the bishop was right at least in this: it would have been impossible, completely and entirely, for any woman to have written the plays of Shakespeare in the age of Shakespeare. Let me imagine, since facts are so hard to come by, what would have happened had Shakespeare had a wonderfully gifted sister, called Judith, let us say. Shakespeare himself went, very probably – his mother was an heiress – to the grammar school, where he may have learnt Latin – Ovid, Virgil, and Horace – and the elements of grammar and logic. He was, it is well known, a wild boy who poached rabbits, perhaps shot a deer, and had, rather sooner than he should have done, to marry a woman in the neighbourhood, who bore him a child rather quicker than was right. That escapade sent him to seek his fortune in London. He had, it seemed, a taste for the theatre; he began by holding horses at the stage door. Very soon he got work in the theatre, became a successful actor, and lived at the hub of the universe, meeting everybody, knowing everybody, practising his art on the boards, exercising his wits in the streets, and even getting access to the palace of the queen. Meanwhile his extraordinarily gifted sister, let us suppose, remained at home. She was as adventurous, as imaginative, as agog to see the world as he was. But she was not sent to school. She had no chance of learning grammar and logic, let alone of reading Horace and Virgil. She picked up a book now and then, one of her brother's, perhaps, and read a few pages. But then her parents came in and told her to mend the stockings or mind the stew and not moon about with books and papers. They would have spoken sharply but kindly, for they were substantial people who knew the conditions of life for a woman and loved their daughter – indeed, more likely than not she was the apple of her father's eye. Perhaps she scribbled some pages up in an apple loft on the sly, but was careful to hide them or set fire to them. Soon, however, before she was out of her teens, she was to be betrothed to the son of a neighbouring wool-stapler. She cried out that marriage was hateful to her, and for that she was severely beaten by her father. Then he ceased to scold her. He begged her instead not to hurt him, not to shame him in this matter of her marriage. He would give her a chain of beads or a fine petticoat, he said; and there were tears in his eyes. How could she disobey him? How could she break his heart? The force of her own gift alone drove her to it. She made up a small parcel of her belongings, let herself down by a rope one summer's night and took the road to London. She was not seventeen. The birds that sang in the hedge were not more musical than she was. She had the quickest fancy, a gift like her brother's, for the tune of words. Like him, she had a taste for the theatre. She stood at the stage door; she wanted to act, she said. Men laughed in her face. The manager – a loose-lipped man – guffawed. He bellowed something about poodles dancing and women acting – no woman, he said, could possibly be an actress. He hinted – you can imagine what. She could get no training in her craft. Could she even seek her dinner in a tavern or roam the streets at midnight? Yet her genius was for fiction and listed to feed abundantly upon the lives of men and women and the study of their ways. At last – for she was very young, oddly like Shakespeare the poet in her face, with the same grey eyes and rounded brows – at last Nick Greene the actor-manager took pity on her; she found herself with child by that gentleman and so – who shall measure the heat and violence of the poet's heart when caught and tangled in a woman's body? – killed herself one winter's night and lies buried at some cross-roads where the omnibuses now stop outside the Elephant and Castle.

women; fiction; gender; discrimination; division of labour; genius

Postlogue

This concluding chapter leads the way from the early 20th century to the landscapes of Theory. The book ends thus because of the 'material' nature of writing. Since the establishment of copyright law in the 18th century, writing is (rightly – and writely –) the intellectual 'property' of the writer. This means that any work which is within copyright (during the lifetime of the author, and for 70 years after his/her death) cannot simply be freely reproduced. Reprinting substantial extracts (apart from in limited circumstances) is subject a) to permission from the copyright owner and b) to the possible payment of a permissions fee. That is as it should be. The Postlogue summarises and quotes from those works still in copyright, with the fervent hope that you will follow them up and read them in full.

The legacy of the 19th century

Matthew Arnold's dictum that culture is 'the best that has been thought and said in the world' continued to reverberate well into the 20th century. In 1924, I. A. Richards added a moral cast to this definition of culture: 'The arts are our storehouse of recorded values.'[1] He believed that these were not merely

---

1   I. A. Richards (1893–1979) *Principles of Literary Criticism (1924)* (Routledge & Kegan Paul, 1961)

storehouses to be kept out of sight, but that 'They record the most important judgments we possess as to the values of experience...' This was echoed in the work of critics and influential university teachers of English, F.R. and Q.D. Leavis. Together with like-minded colleagues, they produced *Scrutiny*, a literary journal which ran for nearly twenty years, between the 1930s and the 1950s.

As the 20th century progressed, critical thinking, in its turn, scrutinised (!) the above assumptions. By the 1930s, a decade of cultural development and political turmoil, there were attempts to 'theorise' the principles behind the literary and practical criticism fostered by the *Scrutiny* group. A short and passionate epistolary exchange took place in its pages between Leavis and Rene Wellek. In 1937 the latter offered a 'theorisation' – ie., an analysis of the principles which lay behind Leavis's critical writing. In a letter headed 'Literary Criticism and Philosophy', Wellek wrote:

> *Allow me to sketch your ideal of poetry, your 'norm' with which you measure every poet: your poetry must be in serious relation to actuality, it must have a firm grasp of the actual, of the object, it must be in relation to life... it should not be personal in the sense of indulging in personal dreams and fantasies, there should be no emotion for its own sake in it...no luxury in pain or joy, but also no sensuous poverty, but a sharp, concrete realisation, a sensuous particularity. The language of your poetry must not be cut off from speech...*

The above echoes some of Wordsworth's 1798 'Advertisement to the Lyrical Ballads', recommending a combination of 'ordinary' speech for poetry, together with keeping emotion at a distance from the compositional process. Leavis's honest and forthright reply to Wellek asserted that literary criticism and philosophy were 'quite distinct and different kinds of disciplines':

> *'My whole effort was to work in terms of concrete judgements and particular analyses…There is, I hope, a chance that I may in this way have advanced theory, even if I haven't done the theorising.*

The difference of opinion with regard to pro-theory and anti-theory (ie., untheorised practice) presaged a debate which still continues, especially within the Creative Writing community. Now it is more likely to be couched as Theory and anti-Theory.

Critical thinking in the second half of the 20th century, influenced by philosophy and linguistics, along with other interdisciplinary intellectual developments, has taken a more trenchant view of, and questioning approach to, culture and the arts. In 1994 Edward Said retrospectively challenged Matthew Arnold on his putative class-based, colonialist belief in the value of culture:

> *…culture is a concept that includes a refining and elevating element…as Matthew Arnold put it in the 1860s. Arnold believed that culture palliates, if it does not altogether neutralise, the ravages of a modern, aggressive, mercantile, and brutalising urban existence…*[2]

While these discussions will doubtless continue, what is not

---

2   *Culture and Imperialism* (Vintage Books, 1994).

in question at the centre of CW is the fact that the 'author', is both an empirical ('real') figure and a theoretical concept.

T(heory)-break

While authorship – in its currently used cultural sense – is the aim of CW (this in itself is a controversial notion),[3] the concept of 'authorship' has been opened up to one of the most exciting discussions in literary/cultural theory. The spur was Roland Barthes' 1967 essay 'The Death of the Author':[4]

> *To give a text an Author is to impose a limit on that text, to furnish it with a final signified, to close the writing. Such a conception suits criticism very well, the latter then allotting to itself the important task of discovering the Author (or its hypostases: society, history, psyche, liberty) beneath the work: when the Author has been found, the text is 'explained' – victory to the critic...the reign of the Author has also been that of the Critic...*
>
> *We know that to give writing its future, it is necessary to overthrow the myth: the birth of the reader must be at the cost of the death of the Author.*

Leaving the critic and reader aside, for the moment, and before the whole edifice of Western authorial knowledge has been dominoed, Sean Burke has saved the day:

> *...albeit antithetically, to remind us of the extent to which*

---

3 See my *The Author is not Dead, Merely Somewhere Else: Creative Writing Reconceived (Palgrave Macmillan 2008).*

4 Roland Barthes, 'The Death of the Author' (1967), in *Image, Music, Text, trans. Stephen Heath* (Fontana, 1977).

> *the history of our thought is bound up with conceptions*
> *of what it means to author a text. With unavoidable*
> *irony, the theory of authorial absence no more signalled a*
> *disengagement with issues of authorship than...negative*
> *theology reflects an indifference to Divinity.*[5]

The author, the imagination and the text

With the day saved, Roland Barthes may return to the discussion, reminding us that '...The author is a modern figure... emerging from the Middle Ages with English empiricism, French rationalism and the personal faith of the Reformation...'[6] Before this, the idea of individual, text-responsible authorship was differently glossed, in large part on the basis of what we now call 'genre':

> *There was a time when the texts that we today call 'literary'*
> *(narrative, stories, epics, tragedies, comedies) were put into*
> *circulation, and valorised without any question about the*
> *identity of their author... On the other hand, those texts that*
> *we now would call scientific – those dealing with cosmology*
> *and the heavens, Medicine and illnesses, natural sciences*
> *and geography – were accepted in the Middle Ages, as 'true',*
> *only when marked with the name of their author...*

The return of this 'modern' concept of author and authorship, has led to certain cultural consequences, which Michel Foucault refers to as the 'author function':

---

5   Sean Burke, *Authorship* (Edinburgh, 1995).
6   Roland Barthes (1915-1980) 'The Death of the Author', in *Image, Music, Text,* translated by Stephen Heath (Fontana, 1977).

...an author's name...performs a certain role with regard to narrative discourse, assuring a classificatory function...to group together a certain number of texts, define them, differentiate them from and contrast them to others. In addition, it establishes a relationship among the texts...of homogeneity, filiation, authentication... the fact that the discourse has an author's name, that one can say 'this was written by so-an-so'...shows that this discourse is not ordinary everyday speech that merely comes and goes...[7]

It is common at readings of imaginative writing (prose and poetry), as well as in interviews on TV and radio, that questions to the author will take the form of 'from where do you get your inspiration/ideas?' 'who inspires you?', even 'who is your favourite author?', as if these might lead to an answer which reveals where it all 'comes from'.

These questions derive in part from the understanding that the language in imaginative writing is, indeed, different from 'ordinary speech'. Is it, therefore, possible to define what kind of person might become an author? Sigmund Freud, responsible for much insight and mis-insight, offered a possible answer, by speculating on a link between childhood and the imaginative writer:

...every child at play behaves like a creative writer, in that he creates a world of his own... The creative writer...creates a world of phantasy...which he invests with large amounts of emotion – while separating it sharply from reality...

---

7   Michel Foucault, 'What is an Author?' In *The Foucault Reader* (ed. Paul Rabinow, Penguin, 1991).

> *many things which…in themselves, are actually distressing,*
> *can become a source of pleasure…*[8]

However, even though there appears to be 'pleasure' in the outcome, it is not untrammelled: '…a happy person never phantasises, only an unsatisfied one. The motive forces of phantasies are unsatisfied wishes…These motivating wishes …are either ambitious wishes, or they are erotic ones. Freud includes emotions as part of his theory of the sources of imaginative writing, and 'emotion', which, as we have seen, was an ongoing 19th-century preoccupation, lies behind more recent pronouncements. T. S. Eliot claims that infusing 'emotion' (of what kind, we don't know) 'in the form of art' is best done by finding an 'objective correlative'; in other words, a set of objects, a situation…The artistic "inevitability" lies in this complete adequacy of the external to the emotion…' This feeds into his 'Impersonal theory of poetry'. Eliot states that '…the more perfect the artist, the more completely separate in him will be the man who suffers and the mind which creates; the more perfectly will the mind digest and transmute the passions which are its material'.[9] Implicitly, this takes us back to Wordsworth's 'emotion recollected in tranquillity'.

Bringing together author, 'inspiration', imagination and text, Sean Burke provides more meaningful questions:

> *Do we dream or are we dreamt?…When an author writes*
> *or thinks to be writing, is that author simultaneously*

8   Sigmund Freud (1856-1939) 'Creative Writers and Day Dreaming' (1907), translated by *I.F. Duff (1887-1957)*, in *The Freud Reader '*, ed. Peter Gay (Vintage, 1989).

9   T.S. Eliot (1888-1965), 'Tradition and the Individual Talent' (1917), in *Selected Essays* (Faber, 1958).

*written? Does creative imagination guide the composition,
or is the writer like the scrawl of an alien power trying
out a new pen? Are the 'great authors' masters in the house
of language, or its privileged tenants? Is the author the
producer of the text or its product? Do we speak language or
does language speak us?*

Burke's list of questions take us to the edge of the written
text. In the 20th century. Ferdinand de Saussure, Swiss linguist
and philosopher, approached language as a social phenomenon,
practically and theoretically. His *Cours de linguistique générale*
was published posthumously in 1916. Roland Barthes succinctly
summarised the three main features which characterise Saussure's
analysis of language as a structural system. *La langue*, language as
an abstract system, which Barthes describes as 'the social part
of language, the individual cannot by himself either create or
modify...' *La parole* (speech), he says, 'is essentially an individual
act of selection and actualisation', that is, the general speech we
use and hear in real life. Finally, *idiolect* is the distinctive cast of
language which belongs to a single individual.[10]

Adding to ideas which flow from *la langue*, is the important
matter of register in language. Richards illustrates this in the
contrast between 'scientific' and 'artistic' language:

*A statement may be used for the sake of the reference, true
or false, which it causes. This is the scientific use of language.
But it may also be used for the sake of the effects in emotion
and attitude produced by the reference it occasions. This is
the emotive use of language...*

---

10   Roland Barthes, *Elements of Semiology (1964)*, trans. Annette Lavers and Colin
     Smith (Jonathan Cape, 1967).

These distinctions are important, not merely to illustrate conceptual subtleties, but because, as Cora Kaplan points out:

> *Language is the most important of all the forms of human communication. Through the acquisition of language we become human and social beings: the words we speak situate us in our gender and our class. Through language we come to 'know' who we are.[11]*

We may be able perfectly well to distinguish between the basic imaginative genres of poetry, stories/novels, drama, but how do we identify what a text 'is'? Roland Barthes' incisive intellect takes nothing for granted, referring to what is known as the theory of intertextuality:

> *…We know now that a text is…a multi-dimensional space in which a variety of writings, none of them original, clash. The text is a tissue of quotations drawn from the innumerable centres of culture…the writer can only imitate a gesture that is always anterior, never original. His only power is to mix writings, to counter the ones with the others, in such a way as never to rest on any one of them.*

Russian philosopher, Mikhail Bakhtin, contributed two further terms to the vocabulary of intertextuality: heteroglossia and dialogisation:

> *…The novel orchestrates all its themes, the totality of the world of objects and ideas depicted and expressed in it, by means of the social diversity of speech type…Authorial*

11   Cora Kaplan, *Sea Changes:Culture and Feminism* (Verso, 1986).

speech, the speeches of narrators, inserted genres, the speech of characters are merely those fundamental compositional unities with whose help heteroglossia can enter the novel; each of them...(always more or less dialogised)...its dialogisation – this is the basic distinguishing feature of the stylistics of the novel. [12]

INTENTION

Much that goes to produce a poem is, of course, unconscious...even if we knew far more than we do about how the mind works, the attempt to display the inner working of the artist's mind by the evidence of his work alone must be subject to the gravest dangers...nearly all speculations as to what went on in the artist's mind are unverifiable...

Thus wrote I.A. Richards in 1924. Nevertheless, the notion of authorial intention permeates CW pedagogy. One might have hoped that the oft-referenced essay on 'The Intentional Fallacy', first published in 1946, would have scotched this particular chimera:

'Intention'... corresponds to what he intended as a formula which more or less explicitly has had wide acceptance... Intention is design or plan in the author's mind.

One must ask how a critic expects to get an answer to the question about intention. How is he to find out what the

12 Mikhail Bakhtin (1895-1975) *The Dialogic Imagination (1975)*, ed. Michael Holquist. Trans. Caryl Emerson and Michael Holquist (University of Texas Press, 1981).

poet tried to do? If the poet succeeded in doing it, then the poem itself shows what he was trying to do.

It would be convenient if the passwords of the intentional school, 'sincerity', 'fidelity', 'spontaneity', 'authenticity', 'genuineness', 'originality', could be equated with terms such as 'integrity', 'relevance', 'unity', 'function', 'maturity', 'subtlety', 'adequacy', and other more precise terms of evaluation – in short, if 'expression' always meant aesthetic achievement. But this is not so.[13]

In the same book, by the same authors, a further two fallacies were listed:

The Intentional Fallacy is a confusion between the poem and its origins, a special case of what is known to philosophers as the Genetic Fallacy...The Affective Fallacy is a confusion between the poem and its results (what it is and what it does), a special case of epistemological scepticism...It begins by trying to derive the standard of criticism from the psychological effects of he poem and ends in impressionism and relativism. The outcome of either Fallacy, the Intentional or the Affective, is that the poem itself, as an object of specifically critical judgement, tends to disappear.

To the Intentional, Affective and Genetic Fallacies, we might add – referring back to the 19th century – the Pathetic Fallacy. This was coined by John Ruskin,[14] in disapproval of the kind of poetic language which projects strong emotion

---

13 W.K. Wimsatt (1907-1975) and Monroe Beardsley (1915-1985). *The Verbal Icon: Studies in the Meaning of Poetry* (Johns Hopkins University Press, 1946).

14 John Ruskin, *Modern Painters* (1946).

onto inanimate objects or creatures – what we would now call anthropomorphising. 'All violent feelings,' he writes, 'have the same effect. They produce in us a falseness in all our impressions of external things, which I would generally characterise as the *Pathetic Fallacy.*'

THE CRITIC AND CRITICISM

Barthes critically commented that '...the reign of the Author has also been that of the Critic...' One might say, how could it have been otherwise, and how could it be otherwise? However, since we have retrieved (even if temporarily) the Author, we can give the Critic some attention.

The 19th-century approach to literary 'appreciation' developed into what came to be called 'literary criticism', applied in relation to the 'creative'. This binary assumption still leads to debate. In 1923, Eliot contested Matthew Arnold's separation of the 'critical' from the 'creative', privileging the former:

> *...he overlooks the capital importance of criticism in the work of creation itself. Probably, indeed, the larger part of the labour of an author in composing his work is critical labour; the labour of sifting, combining, constructing, expunging, correcting, testing: this frightful toil is as much critical as creative. I maintain even that the criticism employed by a trained and skilled writer on his own work is the most vital, the highest kind of criticism; and...that some creative writers are superior to others solely because their critical faculty is superior.[15]*

---

15   T.S. Eliot, 'The Function of Criticism' (1923) in *Selected Essays* (Faber, 1958).

A decade or so later, F. R. Leavis, in his 1937 exchange with Rene Wellek, argued that criticism should be combined with evaluation – making some kind of value judgement – though, as before, there is little sense of the underlying principles of evaluation:

> *The critic's aim is, first to realise as sensitively and completely as possible this or that which claims his attention; and a certain valuing is implicit in the realising. As he matures in experience of the new thing he asks, explicitly and implicitly: 'Where does this come? How does it stand in relation to...? How relatively important does it seem?'*

Terry Eagleton's instrumental approach to the principles of Marxist criticism, lists four kinds. The *anthropological* approach asks: 'What is the function of art within social evolution?... How does art relate to myth, ritual, religion and language, and what are its social functions?' *Political* criticism, deriving from Soviet literature, asks 'whether art should be openly tendentious or "objectively" partisan...*Ideological* criticism asks whether art is 'an embodiment of social ideology or a critique of it?' Finally, the *economic* approach considers 'the material apparatuses of cultural production...theatres and printing presses to literary coteries and institutions of patronage, rehearsing and reviewing to the social context of producers and recipients...' [16]

In 1966, Pierre Macherey pointed out that, because of the essential separation of the creative/critical 'texts', the critical exegesis produced its own, new 'text':

> *Thus, between the writer and the critic, an irreducible*

16   Terry Eagleton, *Marxist Literary Theory.*

difference must be posited right from the beginning: not the difference between two points of view on the same object, but the exclusion separating two forms of discourse... What can be said of the work can never be confused with what the work itself is saying, because two distinct kinds of discourse which differ in both form and content are being superimposed...Let us say, provisionally, that the critic, employing a new language, brings out a difference within the work by demonstrating that it is other than it is...[17]

THE READER

Roland Barthes' project was to try and dispense with both author and critic: 'We know that to give writing its future... the birth of the reader must be at the cost of the death of the Author.' Such sweeping biologism ignores (among other matters) the fact that for the critic to embark on any kind of analytic/evaluative project, s/he has to read the work. Reading, from the way any writer has to read/re-read their text, to the 'innocent' new reader, inevitably has to be at the centre of any critical process.

F.R. Leavis proposed a desirable way of reading: 'Words in poetry invite us not to "think about" and judge, but to "feel into; or become" – to realise a complex experience that is given in the words.' While the connections are not always clear (perhaps because insufficiently 'thought about'?), for Leavis, the link between critic and reader is clear: 'By the critic of poetry I understand the complete reader: the ideal critic is the ideal reader.'

---

17   Pierre Macherey (b. 1938), *A Theory of Literary Production,* trans. Geoffrey Wall (Routledge, 1985).

Wolfgang Iser's influential book of 1976 picks up this desire for an 'ideal reader', by linking it with the perspective of the author, and even with the vexed notion of 'intention': 'An ideal reader would have to have an identical code to that of the author; authors, however, generally recodify prevailing codes in their texts, and so the ideal reader would also have to share the intentions underlying this process.'[18]

Iser's position is, in some ways contradictory. He uses the phrase 'implied reader' – a conceptual term to suggest an abstract reader, not any 'real life' reader. However, the more serious and problematic claim lies in the statement that 'In literary works...the reader "receives" it by composing it.' While the use of the word 'composing' may just suggest a metaphorical gloss, it reveals a claim that the reader, in effect, *becomes* the author; that is, the work only really comes into being by way of the reader. Before that, presumably, the 'work' did not exist in any real or meaningful sense, despite (*pace* Eagleton) it being a part of the nexus of intellectual, imaginative and material production.

Stanley Fish, on the other hand, takes in a broader cultural provenance, with his notion of the *'informed* reader', 'who (1) is a competent speaker of the language out of which the text is built up: (2) in full possession of the semantic knowledge that a mature...listener brings to his task of comprehension... sufficiently experienced as a reader to have internalised the properties of literary discourses, including everything from the most local devices (figures of speech and so on) to whole genres...'[19]

---

18 Wolfgang Iser (1926-2007), *The Act of Reading: a Theory of aesthetic response (1976)*, trans. David Henry Wilson (Johns Hopkins University Press, 1978).

19 Stanley Fish, *Is there a text in this class?* (Harvard, 1980).

Umberto Eco posits a 'model reader', from an inclusive position: taking in the categories of author, intention, text and – by implication – the critic:

> *My idea of textual interpretation as the discovery of a strategy intended to produce a model reader, conceived as the ideal counterpart of a model author (which appears only as a textual strategy), makes the notion of an empirical author's intention radically useless. We have to respect the text, not the author as person so-and-so.*
>
> *I am trying to keep a dialectical link between* intentio operis *and* intentio lectoris. *The problem is that, if one perhaps knows what is meant by 'intention of the reader', it seems more difficult to define abstractly what is meant by 'intention of the text'. The text's intention is not displayed by the textual surface. Thus it is possible to speak of the text's intention only as the result of a conjecture on the part of the reader...* [20]

GENDER, RACE, OTHERNESS AND TRADITION

We return to Matthew Arnold's view of culture, seen through the lens of Edward Said's late 20th century cultural analysis:

> *Now the trouble with this idea of culture is that it entails ...thinking of it as somehow divorced from, because transcending, the everyday world. Most professional humanists as a result are unable to make the connection between the prolonged and sordid cruelty of such practices*

---

20 Umberto Eco (b.1932). *Interpretation and Overinterpretation* (ed. Stefan Collini, CUP, 1992).

as slavery, colonialist and racial oppression, and imperial
subjection on the one hand, and the poetry, fiction, and
philosophy of the society that engages in these practices on
the other... The power to narrate, or to block other narratives
from forming and emerging, is very important to culture
and imperialism.

Apropos of this last point, it should not have escaped the
notice of any reader of this book, that the use of the impersonal
pronoun in the extracts is universally 'he' and 'him'. If it has
escaped the notice of any reader, then this information should
be enlightening and chastening.

Assumptions about, and prejudices deriving from,
gender differences in this Reader may not always be obvious.
Nevertheless, the issue of gender haunts all the fundamental
writerly issues. Freud's controversial point that (effectively)
only unhappy people write imaginatively becomes more
than controversial – even bigoted, one might say, certainly
misogynist – when he comes to allocating 'unsatisfied wishes' by
gender: 'In young women the erotic wishes predominate almost
exclusively...In young men egoistic and ambitious wishes come
to the fore clearly enough alongside of erotic ones.'

From the 18th century onwards, discussions of the nature
of 'genius' were defined by divisive gender-based distinctions:

...Because many of the qualities praised by the advocates
of genius included stereotypically 'feminine' characteristics
(intuition, emotion, imagination, etc.)...a new rhetoric
of exclusion...developed in the eighteenth century...
which gradually grew louder as the nineteenth century
progressed. This rhetoric praised 'feminine' qualities in

male creators…but claimed females could not – or should not – create.[21]

Issues of gender are no longer concealed in the 21st century, and these apply as much to cultural as they do to social and individual matters: '… in western societies (and in other cultures as well) public speech is a male privilege and women's speech restricted by custom in mixed sex gatherings, or, if permitted, still characterised by its private nature, (is) an extension of the trivial domestic discourse of women.'[22] Cora Kaplan traces the 'separate but equal' definition of gender to the mid-19th-century, an 'argument which sometimes tangled with, sometimes included the definition of women's sphere and the development of the true cult of womanhood…Patriarchal dominance involved the suppression of women's speech outside the home and a rigorous censorship of what she could read or write…'

This had vital implications for women as imaginative writers in the past. As Christine Battersby points out: 'The creative woman was an anomaly that simply introduced complications into the patterns of exclusion. A woman who created was faced with a double bind: either to surrender her sexuality (becoming not *masculine*, but a surrogate *male*), or to be *feminine* and *female*, and hence to fail to count as a genius.'

Of course, some things have developed, some things have changed. And yet it is salutary to be reminded of Cora Kaplan's point that the radical – if not revolutionary – consequences of using 'gender difference' as a 'new theoretical approach to literature', will involve 'a profoundly altered view of the relation of both sexes to language, speech, writing and culture…'

---

21 Christine Battersby, *Gender and Genius* (Indiana University Press, 1990).
22 Cora Kaplan, *Sea Changes: Culture and Feminism* (Verso, 1986).

To this must be added other voices:

Postmodernist discourses are often exclusionary, even as they call attention to, appropriate even the experience of 'difference' and 'Otherness' to provide oppositional political meaning, legitimacy and immediacy when they are accused of lacking concrete relevance...Radical postmodernist practice, most powerfully contextualised as a 'politics of difference', should incorporate the voices of displaced, marginalised, exploited and oppressed black people.[23]

In 1917 poet T.S. Eliot formulated a much-quoted powerful statement about cultural tradition:

Tradition...cannot be inherited, and if you want it you must obtain it by great labour. It involves, in the first place, the historical sense...and the historical sense involves a perception, not only of the pastness of the past, but of its presence; the historical sense compels a man (sic) to write not merely with his (sic) own generation in his (sic) bones, but with a feeling that the whole of the literature of Europe from Homer and within it the whole of the literature of his (sic) own country has a simultaneous existence and composes a simultaneous order. This historical sense...makes a writer most acutely conscious of his (sic) place in time, of his (sic) own contemporaneity.'

The challenge, with all the critical thinking in this anthology, and the reading which fans out after and beyond it, is to develop the most far-reaching consciousness of how this moment in

---

23   bell hooks, *Yearning: Race, Gender and Cultural Politics* (Turnaround, (1991).

history (your moment, as you read this) can appropriate and transform Eliot's remark that 'what happens when a new work of art is created is something that happens simultaneously to all the works of art which preceded it'. And, we may add, to what follows it.

Michelene Wandor

FURTHER READING

Each extract in the Reader points the reader to the complete text. The texts quoted in the 'Postlogue' do so similarly. They are all Further Reading, along with the following list.

Literary Theory: a Very Short Introduction, Jonathan Culler (Oxford, 1997, 2000)

Literary Theory: an introduction, Second Edition Terry Eagleton (Blackwell, 1983, 1986)

Textual Intervention, Rob Pope (Routledge, 2003, first pub, 1995).

Exercises in Style, Raymond Queneau, translated by Barbara Wright (New Directions, 1981; first published Gallimard, 1947)

Exploring the Language of Poems, Plays and Prose, Mick Short (Longman, 1996)

Language in Literature: an Introduction to Stylistics, Michael Toolan (Arnold, 1998)

Literature, Peter Widdowson (Routledge, 1999)

Writing in Society, Raymond Williams (Verso 1983, 1991)

On Gender and Writing, edited by Michelene Wandor (Pandora Press, 1983)

Orientalism, Edward Said (2003)

Elements of Style, Strunk and White: first published in 1920, revised in 1959, various editions available.
Intertextuality, Graham Allen (Routledge, 2000)

ENVOI

There's only ever been up for grabs, for theory, a simple trio of knowable, thinkable, zones, corresponding to the three components of the basic model of linguistic communication. There is always, and only ever, a sender, a message, and a received – a writer, a text, a reader – the act of writing, the thing written, the reading of the written thing – the literary input, the literary object found to be 'there', reader(s) attending to this thereness. Or, if you like, cause, consequence, effect. Only three: but a mighty three for all that. And the whole history of criticism, of theorising, is merely a history of the varying, shifting preoccupation across the ages with these three zones, and with these three alone.

(Valentine Cunningham, *Reading After Theory*, Blackwell, 2002, p. 29)

9 781800 465053